PRIMER OF THE COMING WORLD

LEOPOLD SCHWARZSCHILD

Primer of
The Coming World

HAMISH HAMILTON
LONDON

Translated from the German by
NORBERT GUTERMAN

First published 1944

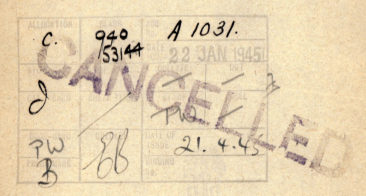

PRINTED IN GREAT BRITAIN BY
MORRISON AND GIBB LTD., LONDON AND EDINBURGH

PREFACE

KAISER WILHELM II of unblessed memory was a perfect dilettante. He was gifted enough to pick up quickly a little something in every field of knowledge. But he was not gifted enough to realize that he did not for that reason understand a great deal. Nor was he modest enough to suspect that in every field the real problem began at the very point where his knowledge and judgment ended. He always took his own sophomoric ideas for grandiose pioneering concepts.

One day he discovered in himself a talented shipbuilding engineer. Once and for all he was going to show the world how a truly modern, perfect, bold, and revolutionary battleship should be built. When his blueprints were ready, he received only non-committal opinions from his experts; so he sent the blueprints to the Italian Admiral Brin, one of the most famous shipbuilders of the day, and asked him for his opinion. The Reich Chancellor preserved the admiral's answer in his memoirs: " The ship which Your Majesty has designed," it ran, " would be the mightiest, the most terrible, and also the loveliest battleship ever seen. It would have a speed which has not yet been attained, its armour would surpass that of anything now afloat, its masts would be the highest in the world, its guns would outrange any others. And the inner appointments are so well arranged that for the whole crew, from the captain down to the cabin boy, it would be a real pleasure to sail in her. This wonderful vessel has only one fault; if she were put in water she would sink like a lump of lead."

We know another wonderful vessel which sank like a lump of lead. It was the world order and world peace of 1919.

Will this happen again? In the course of the next twenty-five years shall we find once more that a new-fangled, daring construction has been erected according to grandiose pioneering ideas—and that it has sunk like a lump of lead?

The danger that this may happen is a real one. It may not emanate from the different governments. Although the period between the two world wars has not raised the credit of governments in this respect, it may be that they have learned more from the experience of the recent past than any individual.

5

At any rate, even in that period, public opinion in the democratic countries was at least as responsible for what happened as their governments. This public opinion was largely created by dilettanti in whose dreams the wonderful vessels were born and who were the originators of absurd undertakings. And while we still know little of the direction in which the true purposes of governments are now moving, the state of present-day public opinion is no mystery. It is not a reassuring state. The old saying: "He has learned nothing and forgotten nothing," is only too often applicable.

One deficiency is particularly striking—surprisingly little is being said about the exact causes for the failure of the previous attempt to establish world peace.

This much is clear: unless we draw up an exact balance sheet of the past, all our projects for the future will inevitably remain dilettantish. World-planners who have no clear idea of the mistakes of 1919 are groping their way in the fog. And unless every new project is scrutinized in the sharp light of past experience, the public will remain in the fog.

Yet it cannot be said that most of the current discussions of war aims take this prime necessity into account. And the reason for this is obvious. There is no body of clear, concrete ideas about the causes of the failure of 1919. The theses about "Versailles," which seemed true for a period of twenty years, have completely collapsed under the impact of events; but there has not been enough time for the formation of new and more correct theses, nor perhaps are people sufficiently flexible in their ideas. Thus the causes of the failure of 1919 are still for many a nebulous subject. They remember an amorphous mass of disproved but not yet quite abandoned facts; of faded but not yet quite buried illusions; of outdated but not yet quite vanished partisan hatreds. No wonder there is no rush to deal with these causes in a really concrete and specific manner. The business of forming exact definitions has never been very popular.

One of the principal intentions of this book is to net the only profit possible from the sad circumstance that the same problem has to be solved for the second time within the life of one generation. I have followed the course of European events at first hand for two decades. I have always been convinced that the true causes of the inexorably progressing disintegration had not the slightest similarity to the legends of international mythology. In my book *World in Trance* I described the course of the drama and analyzed as exactly as I could the causes of the tragedy. In the present book I have tried to apply the specific lessons of the previous settlement to the task confronting the world to-day. These lessons apply to the whole problem from its roots to its last ramifications. The errors of 1919 included some of the most fundamental philosophic premises of the peace as well as numerous purely practical arrangements. Only when we understand that all these things were errors and why they were errors, that we did commit them and how we committed them, will we know the A B C, the beginning of the alphabet, in which the new peace settlement must be written.

And that is not all. The world did not begin in 1919. The nations have demonstrated how they live with each other for thousands of years. This subject, too, is shrouded in fog for all too many minds. To-day more than ever, matters pertaining to international politics are being discussed. A fatal tendency prevails to transfer the experiences of internal domestic politics to international politics—the first and most dangerous source of errors and disappointments. There is also another fatal tendency to consider things only from the point of view of a moralizing, preaching, censuring "it should be," instead of from the point of view of a realistic "it is so," from which all the other phenomena of man and nature are considered. And there are fantastic mythologies and gross mystifications. In this respect, too, I have tried to spell out the elementary A B C. For the most important questions raised by the world settlement I have attempted to clarify the fundamental conditions under which international politics run their course: the forces which they obey, and the limits within which they are confined.

In brief, this book tries to answer the question "why?" Although no exhaustive plan is drawn up here, definite suggestions are made. But the "why" is always the main thing. And this, I think, is what is most needed to-day. The builders of wonderful vessels do not lack enthusiasm and persuasive force. To be able to distinguish between chimerical and practical blueprints one must know the most fundamental rules, experiences, and truths in this field.

Even in an inquiry such as this the ideals of the author must inevitably come to the fore from time to time. Now and then—

although more rarely than is believed—mankind, too, is confronted with alternatives; the choice between them remains free. In such cases there is no other adviser than one's own taste, conscience, and ideals. But these cases are relatively rare. And since my ideals are the traditional ones of the Western world, I need waste very few words on them. I hope I have met the requirement that a book of calm reasonable analysis should be free of declamations, emotionalism, and sentimentalism. There is no lack of declamations, emotionalism, and sentimentalism in the world to-day. What is lacking is their control and rational justification.

I should like to add that this book was written during the summer and fall of 1943. As it goes to press, the world is still in a state of flux. There is a constant stream of new events, conferences, declarations, communiqués, agreements, and protests. I considered for a while whether I should not take cognizance of these most recent happenings in occasional footnotes. I have decided against it. After the publication of this book the stream of new events will continue; but here we deal not with the surface details, but with the forces and causes below the surface. The daily fluctuations of our stormily moving and endlessly changing world absorb too much of our attention in any case, for basically they do not change anything. *Plus ça change, plus c'est la même chose* —"the more it changes, the more it's the same thing."

CONTENTS

The absence of romance in my work will perhaps be disappointing to the reader, but if those who desire to see a true picture of the events which have happened and which, human nature being what it is, are likely to be repeated at some future time with more or less exactness—if they judge that what I have written is useful, then I shall be content.

THUCYDIDES I, 22

PRIMER OF THE COMING WORLD

Part One: The Building Material

CHAPTER ONE

THE OLD ADAM

OLD CLEMENCEAU was convinced that, "essentially, human nature is always the same." Woodrow Wilson was convinced that "human nature has entered a new phase of its development." These two utterly opposite concepts were put forward when the time came to reorganize the world at the end of the last war.

Was this difference of opinion one of those idle philosophical subtleties which arise at the edge of events like foam in the wake of a ship and vanish without leaving a trace? Not at all. The question was an eminently practical one: the nature of the raw material which was to be moulded by the artisans of the new world. The raw material of politics and history is man. What are the properties of this material? What enduring structure can be made out of it? Whenever human society is to be organized anew, the different plans that are proposed must be judged on the basis of their compatibility with human nature.

In many respects the projects put forward in 1919 did not at all fit the species of man known up to that time. No one disputed this. Take the League of Nations, for instance. It was admitted that the League would endure only if men had really become more moral and reasonable than they had been in the past. And many were convinced that they had become so.

What gave them this conviction? Whenever Wilson wanted to justify it he spoke of a new longing that had come into men's hearts. "They desire an entirely new course of action." The existence of new desires, he reasoned, proved that new gifts had emerged. When a new wish is kindled in a man, new capacities necessary for its realization are also born in him.

This reasoning was doubly mistaken. The longing was not

new. And the existence of a longing does not necessarily mean the presence of capacities essential for its realization.

The human longings that manifested themselves toward the end of Kaiser Wilhelm's World War were very old: over and over again they have been aroused in men's hearts.

Prime Minister Hsiang Hsue of the state of Sung lived two and a half thousand years before Wilson. Nevertheless he proposed to the other thirteen Chinese states a covenant for eternal peace; and when he did this he expressed the consuming desires of his contemporaries. The heads of the different governments gathered for a big peace conference and agreed to "abolish war." Hsiang Hsue, the proud initiator of the covenant, was honoured by the gift of sixty-six cities. Incidentally, his best friend tore the letters patent accompanying the gift into shreds. "Your scheme is a delusion," this friend exclaimed. "No offence could be worse than to lead the states astray with such nonsense. You ought to be glad that you have not been punished; why should you be rewarded?" He considered the whole enterprise a veil over the face of truth, a veil more dangerous than the truth itself. And the honourable Hsiang Hsue was so shaken by his friend's arguments that he did not take possession of his sixty-six cities. It should also be mentioned in passing that ten years after its foundation this first League of Nations known to history lay in ruins.

Nor was the desire for world peace absent in the interval between 545 B.C. and A.D. 1919. It manifested itself again and again, in all possible forms, at every conceivable place. It transformed the Roman conquests into the *Pax Romana* and drew these nostalgic words from Saint Augustine: "The Roman Empire was founded by God's consent in order to eliminate war from the world and unite mankind." In the Middle Ages the same longing gave rise to such institutions as the Papal "Truce of God" and the Imperial "Day of Indulgence." After the "wars of religion," which really constituted a world war, it inspired Henry IV of France with his "Great Design" for transforming the Continent into a peaceful federation of states ruled by a "European Senate." After the Napoleonic world war it dictated the text of the Holy Alliance, which introduced collective security against all future wars. One must never be so cautious as when one supposedly discovers something new in man! No, the longing of 1919 was not new.

Even more mistaken was the reasoning that the existence of a longing implied the existence of the capacities necessary to realize it. Thus in Hsiang Hsue's time the longing was there, but the necessary abilities were not, and the enterprise ended in failure. And everyone knows from his own experience that a desire is one thing and the ability to satisfy it something else. How often have you told yourself: "It can't go on this way! From now on . . ." and how often have you been unable to do anything about it!

But the Wilsonians were firm in their conviction, and from the failure of their enterprise one lesson stands out above all others: that all projects for a new world must first be analysed with regard to the question: For what kind of man are they designed? We can divide these projects into two classes: those which assume that the man of to-morrow will be the same as the man of yesterday, and those which assume that between yesterday and to-morrow man will have developed to a higher level.

A wave of idealism and other isms surges around you threateningly when you try to make up your mind on this question. I recall a French naval officer for whom the hull of his submarine had been what a hermitage was for the ancients: a refuge for endless studies and meditations. He insisted on considering this question of human nature against the background of millions of years: what an enormous road we had travelled since Neanderthal man! Why not the same development in the future? No faintheartedness when it comes to man!

Frankly speaking, what we know of Neanderthal man is his skeleton; anything more is only guesswork or fiction. The character of this ancestor of ours—if he was our ancestor—is unknown to us. We do not know what development the nature of *Homo sapiens* has really undergone since the ice age. Even less do we know what development our descendants will go through in an equally long period in the future. Perhaps they will not develop at all. Our universe offers only a few examples of perpetual growth. Most living beings develop up to a certain level and stop there.

But for our purpose we fortunately need not and must not take the coming millions of years into account. We must think of the people of 1950 and 1970. What interests us is the possible transformation of human character during the modest space of a few decades. And to gauge this we have comparative material accumulated during the last four to five thousand years. Has mankind changed during these few thousand years?

One source of confusion must be eliminated at the outset. Obviously man has been able radically to transform his environment. His technology has perfected almost everything outside himself. But what has he been able to perfect within himself? These two entirely different spheres are only too often confused; but we must carefully distinguish between them. As to the nature of man: when and how has it progressed, as is claimed, in the course of our historical experience? About 400 B.C. Thucydides, the "Father of History," explained why he wished to record the events of his time. He wanted to give, he wrote, "a true picture of the events which have happened and which, human nature being what it is, are likely to be repeated at some future time with more or less exactness." And have they not, human nature being what it is, really been repeated over and over again? Whoever considers the destiny of man in the course of these thousands of years cannot help concluding that his character has been confined within the limits of a certain minimum and a certain optimum. Within these limits there have always been variations. Things have swung pendulum-like from the minimum to the optimum and back again, back and forth, over and over. But never has human nature gone beyond these limits, and it has always swung back from the optimum limit sooner or later.

If anything has been transformed, what is it? The instincts? What instincts? All of them obviously remain as they always have been and continue to conflict with one another. Love and hatred dwell in us and confront us every day, sometimes arising from rational causes, sometimes without any relation to any discoverable rational cause. Along with the desire for peace there is the imperious urge for conflict; beside the longing for permanence, the longing for change. Human souls thirst to erect altars, and then to destroy them. They want both to rule and to be ruled. They are driven by conformity and by individualism. The fevers of power, of fame, and of plunder are rampant, and so are the paralyses of cowardice and lethargy. No impulse that has ever existed is lacking to-day and no new impulse has been added to the old ones. Such has been our experience of man's instincts.

Shall we say that our ethics have improved? There are the

books of the Old Testament. However one may interpret them, it will not be denied that they are very old and that they are full of ethical postulates. But which one of these postulates is violated less often to-day than it was at the time the Old Testament was written? These books define sins and crimes. Are there any that are not committed to-day just as they were then? Can it even be maintained that a larger part of humanity is living to-day in the spirit of these ethics? Hardly. The commandments: "Thou shalt not kill," "Thou shalt not steal," "Thou shalt not bear false witness," and "Thou shalt not covet " were not spoken in a vacuum—they were generally accepted moral standards even then. But people sinned against them—just as people sin against them to-day.

Finally, can we claim that human intelligence has improved? The truth is that the experiences of former generations have never taught anything to their descendants. In the days of antiquity men were just as wise as they are to-day, and just as stupid. After having been the arbiter of Europe for three decades, the Swedish Chancellor Axel Oxenstierna was not impressed with the intelligence of governments. He is said to have answered a complaining letter of his son, who represented him at the peace conference after the Thirty Years' War, with the following words: "*An nescis, mi fili, quantilla prudentia mundus regatur?*"—"Do you not know, my son, with what little wisdom the world is governed?" And yet it took one hundred and fifty years from that world war to the next, not twenty! We cannot see any increased wisdom on the part of those who govern the world. Although now and then more enlightened minds have emerged, the sum and the average remain pretty much the same.

There is a legend that, by virtue of some mysterious inspiration, those who are governed are wiser than those who govern them. But no evidence substantiates this. As a rule, those below display no more and no less enlightenment than those above, nor does their intelligence give any proof of progress. The most absurd prejudices are still rampant among groups, classes, and nations; when one becomes obsolete, it is replaced by another. In the course of time different sections of mankind have reeled from one persecution to another. With the same stupidity and the same enthusiasm, inflamed by the same kind of maniacs, they have slaughtered minorities: Christians, witches, Protestants, Catholics, aristocrats, bourgeois, Jews, and what not.

Men's minds are as susceptible as ever to crazy doctrines and chimerical promises, and the opportunities for charlatans, zealots, and gangsters to do their dastardly work are still numerous. According to one author, "the cause of the ruin of democracies" is the credulity of the people when faced with "the insolence of demagogues who flatter and mislead the multitude." The demagogue procliams that "ancient customs must be done away with; ancient ties, civil and sacred, must be broken; everything must be changed according to new and false theories." When he gets into the saddle, "spies and informers are his principal instruments. War is his favourite occupation, for the sake of engrossing the attention of the people and making himself necessary to them as their leader." Who was the author of this exact description? His name was Aristotle, and he lived two thousand three hundred years ago. Such were conditions in his time, and such they have been again and again ever since.

Let us make a wide detour around the swamp of alluring improbabilities. It is improbable that human nature has changed during these last thousands of years, and it is more improbable that it will suddenly change to-morrow. Those who abandoned themselves to such optimism in 1919 may still be excused. They stemmed from a golden age. The nineteenth century, the century of liberalism, marked a pendulum swing toward the optimum limit throughout the world. Once again the illusion could arise then that there were neither limits nor swings of a pendulum. We, however, have been reminded of these limits !

There is an entirely different problem: what can be made of the real human raw material, such as it is and always has been? It is perhaps possible to shape something better out of this material even though its characteristics are still the same. But this problem has nothing to do with the previous one. New possibilities may be investigated and discussed if we start with a sober premise. But if we start with an illusory premise the path leads only to nonsense and bankruptcy. And I think that at least on the problem of human nature there is a good prospect that wide agreement will be reached. After all, everyone is to some extent an expert on this problem.

We can agree that *the raw material of the new world is not a new Adam, but the old Adam.*

CHAPTER TWO

RELATIONS AMONG STATES

STATES ARE COMPOSED of old Adams. They are led by old Adams. It is understandable, therefore, that the relations among states are not very different from what they have always been.

Many people find it much less understandable that as a rule these relations are so bad. Beyond doubt they are much worse than the relations among individuals. The difference is often exaggerated, and from many popular descriptions one might think that perpetual hell prevails in international life. Yet many states have for generations lived with each other just as well as individuals. But wars have always existed, and even aside from wars there is among states a greater degree of immorality than among individuals. More outrages are committed and more decencies neglected. To follow one's own interests exclusively is not exceptional behaviour; but only states go so far as to canonize such behaviour as "*sacro egoismo*" or "isolationism" or what not. Statesmen who are scrupulously honest in their private lives act in their official capacities according to quite different ethical concepts.

This has been explained as the persistence in the field of international politics of a kind of atavistic morality. At all times much thought has been devoted to the problem of making the relations between states more moral. How, in particular, could the morality of statesmen be improved? How shall we make sure that in the exercise of their office they observe the same elementary standards they observe as individuals? All these speculations have produced few answers and few results.

Some of the answers are based on class considerations; there are reformers who persuade themselves and others that all the evil stems from the fact that the statesmen belong to some rotten class—the old school ties of an oligarchy or aristocracy or bourgeoisie. This theory has been tested often enough—but never successfully. No one could maintain seriously that the various historical class changes have led to the emergence of nobler dynasties of statesmen.

Others have pinned their hopes on the individual improvement of statesmen. Almost two hundred years ago Edmund Burke admonished young British statesmen: "to rear to the most perfect vigour and maturity every sort of generous and honest feeling that belongs to our nature; and to bring the dispositions that are lovely in private life into the service and conduct of the Commonwealth, so to be patriots and not to forget we are gentlemen." An admirable admonition which was not without success on British soil! But in the international field one must unfortunately always reckon with the other fellow. The events on the international chessboard result from the moves not of one man, but of several men. Bismarck used a famous image. He, who had been rather gluttonous for ten years, but decidedly satiated for the following twenty, complained of the presence of "pikes in the European carp pond." One pike compels all the carps to live by pike morality.

In Wilson's time another moral hope flourished. Obviously the President himself considered statesmen an incurably cynical race. He built his new structure on the morality of the people at large, the plain men. "I am satisfied that if necessary I can reach the people over the heads of their rulers." They would no longer tolerate anything evil. This was a myth. The present state of the world shows how complete a myth it was.

No, morality has not changed the nature of international politics. Moralistic approaches and expectations have always ended in disappointments. In isolated cases and situations moralistic appeals and pressures have been to some extent beneficent. But on the whole they have been a failure. And there is a good reason for this. It is that the deficiency of morality in this field is not a cause but an effect. Normally, international conditions are not produced by bad morality; bad morality is produced by international conditions.

It is not difficult to discover what distinguishes relations among individuals from relations among states. Consider yourself and your fellow men. Our parents, our churches, and our schools have taught us how to behave morally toward each other. This does not ensure that we really do behave in that way. Anyone will grant that our souls and consciences are unable by themselves to create and preserve our morality. Something else is required, and that something has two aspects: No one among us can employ physical force against the others. We have not the means for it. A power placed above us can employ naked physical force against all of us. It has overwhelming means for this purpose.

Absence of any physical power worth mentioning below, presence of overwhelming physical power above: these are the two foundations on which our social life rests. And they guarantee the observance of certain moral standards. These are not the ideal, Biblical standards—they are more modest ones, defined in the form of laws. Even laws are sometimes successfully violated; but, as a rule, only to the extent to which they can be violated by the naked hand or the hand with the revolver. Beyond this the criminal cannot go. When his revolver-shot produces the inevitable consequences, he cannot resort to cannon. If his individual act sets in motion many avengers, he cannot raise companies or battalions against them. He cannot imprison people or drive them into slavery. On the path of individual crime the second or certainly the third step is barred. For this reason, as a rule few take the first step. You and your neighbour are both compelled to observe elementary morality toward each other, and you and your neighbour can be fairly sure that elementary morality will be observed toward you. Thus a certain minimum level of morality is established in the life of individuals, and on this basis a certain amount of subtler, more voluntary morality can be built.

But we must never forget what makes for this condition. Ultimately not even laws and courts are its basic elements. They themselves have only a borrowed force. The basic element is this dual fact: the complete disarmament of individuals, and the exclusive possession of armed force by an authority above them.

In the relations among states these two fundamental conditions are exactly reversed. Each state possesses all possible weapons, and there is no armed power above it. Each state can commit any crime against other states which it thinks it is in a position to commit. Each state must fear all sorts of crimes on the part of other states unless it has previously rendered them materially incapable of committing them. There is no compulsion to observe the most elementary morality, and no confidence that it will be observed. How can relations among states be compared to relations among individuals?

The fact that in the field of international relations power exists below and impotence above is the key to their history.

By now everyone knows that bandits, madmen, and megalo-maniacs take advantage of this for their own purposes of war and plunder. The "anarchy" in which the states live is cited in every third editorial to-day. But even aside from war the consequences of this state of affairs are of capital importance. Because of it treaties among states are unreliable; they all contain the unwritten clause: "As long as it suits us." Because of it states are com-pelled to take actual measures of defence against remote, hypo-thetical dangers. Much less than individuals, who are protected by the force above them, can they afford to wait; they must often initiate a policy of forestalling a danger which is only a vague possibility. As a result, more decent states are forced to adopt the methods of less decent states. Just as the speed of a convoy is determined by the slowest ship, the degree of morality in international rivalries is often determined by the most immoral state.

Take the case of Constantinople. For two hundred years Russia angled for this strategically situated Turkish city, while Britain did everything in her power to frustrate the Russian designs. The case is a good illustration of how the mechanism works and where it leads.

What motivated the British? Fear! They thought that Russia would not spare them any blow she had the power to deal them, and a foothold in Constantinople would have given her such power. As masters of the straits, the Russians would have had access to the Mediterranean. They might have organized a strong fleet there. This fleet might have allied itself with another Mediterranean fleet. These united fleets might then have under-taken a crushing act of force against Great Britain. This was only a remote possibility, but can a state, which must rely only upon itself for protection, afford to wait? No, it must anticipate, and long before the last stage it must bar the way to any conceivable danger. And so began that century-long Anglo-Russian struggle over Constantinople—to prevent an eventuality remote to the fourth degree.

This struggle had far-reaching consequences. Once it exploded into open war. Several times the two countries were on the brink of war, but most of the time the struggle remained subterranean, almost invisible, confined to the sphere of international politics. Whatever the two countries did in the international field was almost always influenced by this struggle; it was often actually determined by it. Neither power was scrupulous about its means. When the Russians took detours to reach their objective, the British took counter-detours. When one nation used tricks and disloyalties and brutalities, the other could not avoid doing the same. Treaties were broken; new states were brought into the world with the help of forceps; revolutions and counter-revolutions were encouraged. And the ripple created by this rivalry steadily widened its circles; allies were enlisted by both parties, and then again allies against the allies. These had to be supported in their own dubious enterprises, to compensate them for their support. There were cabals, complications, crises, and wars between other states in other zones, caused to a considerable extent by the Anglo-Russian struggle over Constantinople. Let us avoid the usual exaggerations, generalizations, and over-simplifications, however; not all that took place was horrible, much of it remained respectable, and much that was not respectable did no harm to anyone, because the moves and counter-moves cancelled one another. And the intrigues around Constantinople are typical of international relations.

All this should not surprise us nor fill us with righteous indignation against statesmen. We cannot fail to see that our own life history would have been filled with black pages if we had to live under the conditions characterizing the relations among states. In the same "anarchy" we would behave as the states do. If we sensed even the remotest danger and we should always be surrounded by dangers—we should obviously be compelled to forestall it at any cost, by any means. The fact that we are simultaneously living two completely different kinds of lives should not lead us into confusing one with the other. In his life as an individual the old Adam is disarmed, while the community is armed. As a result he is relatively domesticated. In his life as a member of the state these conditions are reversed, and as such he is not domesticated. What is surprising is not that international morality is so often different from individual morality, but that in spite of everything the two are so often identical. That any elements originating in individual morality should penetrate into international conduct is really well-nigh miraculous. From the point of view of pure logic, the conditions of international life are compatible only with what is called " power politics."

"Power politics" is an expression laden with condemnation. With what contempt it was used in 1919! As a matter of fact, it would be as accurate to speak of the "politics of not being overpowered." We should be much happier to-day if between 1933 and 1939 there had been a greater measure of "politics of not being overpowered," and if the instinct to practise this most elementary kind of politics had not been so grievously weakened. "Power politics" and the "politics of not being overpowered" are so interwoven that they can be kept apart only in exceptional cases.

The important question, however, is not what we should condemn, but what we should expect. There are many things that we condemn but that will not vanish simply because we condemn them. In 1919 there was no conflict of moral judgments: there was a conflict of prognoses. On one side were those who thought "that we are on the threshold of a new age," that from then on it was possible to organize international relations without any "power politics." Opposing them was stubborn Clemenceau, who insisted that "essentially the old order does not change" and that "the politics of power are inevitable." Now that his forecast has proved correct for twenty years, people are again asking what we can expect! This is indeed a strange world.

The question can be answered clearly. Only in one single case could we rely on the emergence of a new kind of international relations: if all the powers, without exception, were subjected to the power of a completely irresistible world authority. It would have to be a world authority incomparably more powerful, dominant, and irresistible than the League of Nations of 1919. The physical power this world authority could wield against any state would have to be as overwhelmingly superior as the state authority is to-day with regard to every individual. The establishment of such a world authority would be the most extraordinary event in world history. I shall discuss in the latter part of this book whether and to what extent such a world authority is possible, probable, and desirable.

Whatever the answer to these questions, this much is certain: only in this extreme case would we be justified in expecting a drastic change in international relations. But no half-solution, no intermediate course, can give us this confidence. So long as all states are not at least subjected to the same compulsion, so long as they do not enjoy the same security as you and I, the peculiar features of international life will continue. Half-compulsion is no compulsion at all. Half-security is not security. Short of complete compulsion and complete security the mechanism will turn as before, and no morality, no mysticism, will induce it to run in reverse. Let us guard ourselves from putting our faith in any new promises as insubstantial as those of 1919. Nothing would be more fatal than to follow once again the *fata morgana* that in the post-war world the states will be pervaded by a morality different from the present one.

We can agree that *as long as an irresistible super-authority does not keep all states under compulsion and guarantees the security of all of them, the character of international relations will remain unchanged.*

Part Two : The World Authority

CHAPTER THREE

WHAT KEEPS THE GUARDIANS IN AGREEMENT?

ONCE AGAIN THE minds of men are turning to the establishment of such a world authority over the various states.

In examining the various ideas proposed one is startled to discover that the most logical and consistent idea is as good as left out of the discussion. The most logical and consistent idea would, of course, be to do away with the states altogether and to create the "United States of the World," with one territory, one government, one army, one law. This would surely abolish all wars and many other plagues.

But people refuse to be logical, and even Woodrow Wilson exclaimed on one occasion: "I don't give a damn about logic!" People simply do not want a world state. Even the eternal peace which it promises does not make it attractive to them.

Naturally, they resist when the attempt is made to force it upon them by violence and conquest. They resisted Napoleon. They resist Hitler even more, although even in the mud which fills his brain an idea vegetates that ultimately he serves the cause of world peace—a quite peculiar type of world peace, to be sure: "a peace founded by the victorious sword of a people of overlords, which puts the world to the service of a higher culture."

But not only is the idea of a world state imposed by force disliked. Even the idea of establishing it peacefully, contractually, by general consent, obviously lacks appeal. Even the makers of post-war projects—who do not easily shrink from anything— avoid this most summary, most perfect of all projects. It has no prospect of being accepted—at least not during the settlement of to-morrow. Perhaps at some later date, in the remote future. To-day the 450,000,000 Chinese, as well as the 4,500,000 Swiss and every other nation, would reject any proposal to amalgamate them into a world state. It is not even worth while discussing the matter. Many things which seem rationally perfect are not worth while speaking about.

Thus at the very outset we are left with a much weaker alternative: the possibility of realizing the desired goal through the co-operation of a number of independent states. A number of governments or nations would undertake to perform the mission of guardians.

Now, this could be arranged in all sorts of ways. Of what nations, for instance, should the super-authority be formed? Of only the most powerful? This was done in 1815 in the Holy Alliance. Or of as many as possible? Such was the League of 1919. Which of the two is better?

Then there is the question of how to organize the co-operation of the participants. The Holy Alliance had no special machinery or statutes. It consisted merely in the agreement of the four participants to discuss with one another all dangerous occurrences and to determine the necessary steps to be taken. The League of Nations, for similar discussion and decisions, had an elaborate machinery and a detailed covenant. Which of the two is more practical?

Another question: shall all the participants have an equal voice in the decisions? Then Norway would have the same influence as China, which has one hundred and fifty times as many people. Or shall the ballots be proportionate to the size of each country? Then China would have three times more influence than the United States.

These are all points which in 1919 caused many headaches. And there are others just as knotty. Once again they offer the possibility of debates and endless ingenious projects. But, without underestimating questions of secondary importance, let us be clear at once that all these questions *are* of secondary importance. What importance, for instance, has the question of who will be the wielders of the super-authority? The popular instinct is characteristically simple in this matter. It speaks of the "big three"—it considers the United States, the British Commonwealth, and the Soviet Union as the future guardians. Frequently China is added, and one has the "big four." Occasionally, also, a regenerated France is included. In any case, the popular idea is that the Atlas who will support the globe will be composed of a very small number of first-rank powers. This idea happens to be correct. Everything will actually depend on the big powers— and however many smaller powers are nominally incorporated into the super-authority will not make any considerable difference.

Among the many illusions of 1919 there was the one about the small states. Wilson considered that one of the strongest features of his League of Nations was the fact that the small states would have the same voting rights in it as the big ones. He thought that together they would constitute a mighty weight. And he considered them a weight on the side of good; just as he considered the little men nobler than the big men, he considered the little states nobler than the big states. This was a double chimera. Small states, like small men, are neither nobler nor less noble than big ones; their nobility or lack of nobility must be confined to a smaller domain. Moreover, the little powers in the League did not turn out to be the big weight they were supposed to be. Despite their large number and their equal right to vote, they turned out to be of no weight taken all together. For in great world questions small states as a rule lack not only the opportunity but even the will to play any part of their own. When leonine strength is required, the little ocelots do not coalesce into an independent pack capable of measuring itself against the lions. Some of the ocelots range themselves behind those lions which they have chosen as their protector; others disappear into the caves of non-commitment. In Geneva, when weighty resolutions were to be taken, the smaller states never independently and unitedly defended a thesis. Some of them voted with England, others with France, others, if worst came to worst, with Italy—and some did not vote at all.

Such is the role of the lesser states when important questions are the order of the day. The effectiveness or ineffectiveness of the "world council" will be essentially the same whether it is formed only of the "big three" or "big four" or whether in addition to these a greater or smaller number of lesser states belong to it. And this is typical of all the questions which seem to be of the first order, but actually are only secondary.

The questions of the first order are of an entirely different kind. Unfortunately there is a tendency to give them only casual, fleeting recognition.

To broach the first and most portentous of these questions: is there any guarantee that the members of the world council will continue to be in harmony? Co-operation without agreement is obviously unthinkable. As soon as agreement among the guardians on aims and principles is gone, the council must be paralysed, to all intents and purposes. There will no longer be any resolutions, only pseudo-resolutions at the very best. World events will take their course completely outside the influence of the immobilized super-authority.

Now what reliance can we have in the permanent harmony of the "big three" or "big four?" The question is formulated exactly. It does not ask what will happen, but on what we can reasonably rely. We are not prophets. In that domain of the incalculable called history no one can make long-term prophecies. We cannot know what will happen many years or decades from now. But there are things on which one can rely with normal caution, and there are things on which one cannot normally rely. What reliance can we place on continued agreement among the guardians?

Last time, expectations in this direction were jubilant. The participants had gone through the hardest possible school. A terrible apocalypse had taught them that without unity they were doomed. In fire and blood and through indescribable sufferings their unity had been forged. The sacred pledge to persevere from now on in unity was written on parchment and solemnly signed. Wilson considered it "a definite guarantee." Millions shared his opinion. But in reality disagreement had re-entered the scene even before the Covenant was signed. Not only did America in the end refuse to participate in the League— or, in other words, refuse even to promise to agree; even more portentous was the fact that the great powers which did participate were profoundly disunited from the very beginning. On at least one capital question the purposes of Great Britain and France were diametrically opposed. The French wanted Germany to remain militarily impotent. The British wanted Germany to recover her military power in order to counterbalance France's power. We know what followed. From this primary disunity arose secondary and tertiary disunities. The League could not steer any clear-cut course; it lay firmly anchored in port and rotted.

Such was the experience of this attempt to maintain unity. Even the first prerequisite for making the super-authority workable was lacking. Unity was by no means realized in the present; still less was it assured for the future. It was not created and preserved by the treaty in which it was solemnly pledged, nor by the immense desire for it which seized mankind after the Armistice, nor by the close coalition formed during the war in

whose lasting unifying effect so many people believed. Unity
against something for which the war coalition had been formed
did not by any means give rise to unity for something which was
necessary for post-war co-operation. And did war coalitions
ever end differently?

It would be an understatement to say that war coalitions
have only seldom been prolonged into solid post-war alliances.
In recent centuries the unity realized during a war has always
been shattered after a few years of peace; the longest period such
unity has lasted seems to have been ten years. The subsequent
disunity often resulted in wars between countries which only
the day before had been allied. In 1864 Prussia and Austria
together made war against Denmark. Two years later they were
fighting each other. There is no exception to the rule that countries
united in a war coalition quickly lose their harmony once the
war is over, and enter upon divergent paths. With the Allies
of 1918 this harmony lasted less than a year, although the fact
was not officially recognized. The Allies of 1815 were so disunited after seven years that they even recognized the fact
officially; after the suicide of Foreign Secretary Castlereagh,
Great Britain notified her partners of her withdrawal from the
Holy Alliance, and the others disintegrated. And it is instructive
in more than one respect to recall the only full-fledged alliance
ever entered into by the United States.

This was the alliance concluded during the catastrophic
months of Valley Forge between Benjamin Franklin and the
ministers of Louis XVI. The French and Americans were motivated not by common interests *pro*, but by common interests
contra. The King himself said this with a frankness which deserves
respect. France entered the war, drawing Spain and Holland
in with her. For the space of five years she diverted almost the
entire military might of Great Britain on land and on sea toward
herself. For these five years, moreover, she functioned as the
arsenal and treasury of American democracy. In 1783, when
England was forced to swallow the bitter pill and recognize
America's independence in the Treaty of Paris, it was clear
enough that she had been defeated principally by France. And
although the American revolutionaries hated nothing more than
monarchies and despotisms, enthusiasm prevailed among them
toward France. They felt that France and America were forever
united. Their alliance—or at least parts of it—was valid beyond

the war. And even stronger and less perishable than the letter of the alliance seemed their common interests.

Came the French Revolution. The Kingdom was followed by the Republic, and the monarchs formed a coalition against it. "*Contre nous de la tyrannie l'étendard sanglant est levé*," sang the French when their new, now revolutionary, war with England began. In 1793 it was they who needed help. They recalled their revolutionary brothers in America, the alliance, the unity of purpose. But after ten years the unity had evaporated. Washington's policy was now reconciliation with England. He proclaimed America's neutrality. Just as Franklin had been sent to Paris, now Citizen Genet was sent to America by the French in their need. He came with demands which were far from excessive; he did not ask, with the treaty of alliance in hand, for American armed assistance. All he asked for was a friendly attitude on certain maritime questions. But even that proved too much. When Citizen Genet addressed himself directly to the American public—"prodded the public," as we might say to-day—he was sent home. Instead of co-operation, a naval war developed between the two states.

A heated discussion continued for decades over the question whether America had not broken her treaty, or at least her obligations of gratitude. But this question does not concern us here; what is important is the fact that the two states, ten years after their war coalition, no longer pulled at the same end of the rope, but at opposite ends, until in 1812 the situation was reversed again. And what must be particularly emphasized is the little detail that the American republicans and revolutionaries were closely united with the Bourbon monarchy and autocracy; that they completely dissociated themselves from the French Republic and Revolution; and that later they again made common cause with the Napoleonic monarchy and dictatorship. As frequently before and after in the field of international politics, the colour of the various regimes had no great influence. Ideological similarity did not necessarily lead to unity, nor did ideological dissimilarity necessarily lead to disunity. It is timely to keep this in mind to-day, for many among us like to consider all the questions of the post-war world only from the point of view of the sympathies and antipathies existing between Soviet Russia and the West. Do we want a world peace authority? Nothing is easier if only the antipathies toward our partner

Russia cease. Is unity necessary among the members of the council? Nothing will ensure it more firmly than if here and now we stop our anti-Bolshevist talk. But in fact all this is not so simple. The permanent unity of the "big three" or the "big four" would be insecure even if such a thing as Bolshevism did not exist at all. The roads of even ideologically identical allies have never failed to diverge after a war.

Such, then, is our experience. The plan according to which the post-war world will have to be constructed will depend upon whether or not we can expect the suggested super-authority to function. And this again depends upon whether we can or cannot expect the future guardians to remain in permanent agreement. We know from experience that such agreement is not perpetuated by treaties, or by the emotion of the moment, or by goodness, self-control, insight, or reason. Special means never applied before must be invented to perpetuate something that has never before remained permanent. We cannot expect it to happen by some unprecedented miracle.

The consistent ease with which this fact is glossed over is disquieting. In the current debates what is the most glaring weakness in all the projects for establishing a world authority seems to be accepted as a secure base for it. Moreover, there are fanatics who denounce every doubt that is raised as sabotage, splitting tactics, and defeatism. According to them, anyone who does not believe blindly in the continued unity of the nations now united in war gives aid and comfort to the enemy. But we must not become confused on this point. The force that has preserved unity during the fighting is the enemy; and the meaning of victory is precisely to break the force which has created this unity. Unity after victory is something entirely different from unity before victory. Any insight into the reality of the post-war world is barred to us if this fact remains veiled. "Solutions" that do not even take into account the hub of the problem are not solutions, but phrases, invitations to gambling. Let us be warned by the consequences of the gambling of 1919.

We can agree that *no world authority consisting of independent states is reliable so long as means are not discovered for ensuring the continued agreement of its members.*

CHAPTER FOUR

THE TRAGIC MILITARY DILEMMA

IS THERE ANY METHOD of reliability cementing the unity of the guardians?

Certainly there is! But it is like a red-hot iron—no one will willingly grasp it. Although it is the only possible method, most of the project-makers make a wide detour around it. And that is not surprising considering its nature.

Let us restate the two determining factors in international relations. All the states have physical power, and no physical power exists over them. Only if these two factors are turned into their opposites will this condition be changed. All military power —armies, navies, and air fleets—must be taken away from the members of the world council and transferred to the world council itself. The separate military establishments of the guardians— that is to say, the United States, the British Commonwealth, and Soviet Russia—must be given up. They must be cartellized into one single military machine controlled by the super-authority. Then and only then can we reasonably expect that a certain measure of unity of purpose will prevail among its members, that a common policy will be formulated on every occasion, and that the resolutions taken will always be carried out.

Why this is so must be clear by now; one glance at our life as individuals within the state explains it. The domesticated condition under which the individual is disarmed and the state is armed encourages unity. Unbridgeable divergencies among the various Joneses and Smiths arise less frequently; because they can do evil and must fear evil only within certain narrow limits, their aims do not become so frequently antagonistic. Even if they do become so, the effect of domestication is that their differences can in the end be smoothed out. The Smiths and Joneses usually stop a few steps short of the limit of disagreement and reach a *modus vivendi*. And even if they fail to agree, the conflict of their wills can be controlled notwithstanding. The omnipotence above uses one of its various instruments to force upon the disputants decent behaviour, if not the spirit of unity. If the big powers were in the same position as the Joneses and

Smiths, we should not be worried about their future agreement,
nor about many other questions.

The forty-eight States of the U.S.A. are in this position.
No one among them has any military power of its own to speak
of. Over them is the crushingly superior—in fact, monopolistic—
military might of the Union. The very existence of the United
States rests on these two dry facts. Their influence is not visible,
but concealed, latent. Under normal circumstances the common
man does not notice them and does not realize their enormous
importance. As a rule he considers the good sense of its citizens
the key to the preservation and the proper functioning of the
Union.

But here, as elsewhere, the good sense of the members would
not have been sufficient to maintain their co-operative functioning
for very long. I submit that the picture of a U.S.A. composed
of heavily armed states with a disarmed central authority is
terrifying. There would be the repetitions of 1861 and we dare
not ask ourselves what would be the state of the Union. Just to
illustrate our point, let us consider only what would have
happened to the U.S. Senate in such a case. Obviously the
Senate is for the forty-eight states what the world council would
be for the nations. Now, how would the Senate function if the
states were armed and the Union disarmed? In all probability
it would function miserably. Conflicts would be multiplied, and
they would be more stubborn, more irreconcilable, more confused, more chaotic. Deadlocks which would prevent various
proposals from even reaching the voting stage would be common.
And if something were decided upon, how many of the outvoted
states would carry out a resolution they did not favour if there
were no force over them? It is doubtful whether there would
still be a Congress at all, whether there would still be a United
States.

Few people realize that military power is of such importance.
Our minds rebel against endowing it with so much influence
outside its own limited field, war. Why, we ask, should normal,
civilian life be subjected to the influence of this alien factor?
And our minds rebel even more against ascribing any good
influence to military power. How, we ask, can the force which
serves to kill, destroy, and possibly enslave, be also a force in
the service of law and justice, order, integration, and unity?

It can be and it is. Military power plays the same role in

social relations as gravitation plays in things physical. To be sure, gravity causes a great deal of damage. When a bridge collapses, when a boy drowns in the ocean, when a bomb hits your house and yourself—all this is the work of gravity. But the fact that your house and your table and your bed stand firmly, that you yourself can walk securely, that our ships sail and bring us goods, and that the rain falls and makes the grain for our bread grow—all this is the work of gravity, too. Like gravity, military power acts continuously, ubiquitously, in a thousand ways. The two sometimes bring catastrophes upon us, and it is on these occasions that we notice them. But more frequently—and less noticeably—the two are beneficent. They cause and maintain and stabilize things which are absolutely vital to us. And neither of the two can simply be thought away. Without military power the human world would sink into absolute chaos, as would the world of matter without gravity. We cannot do without either. All we can do is try to make them serve us, to increase their usefulness and decrease their harmfulness as much as possible.

For two hundred years the liberal tradition has been distinguished by resolute blindness to the beneficent aspects of military power. Arms and armed force have always been identified by this tradition with sin and evil. The first angel mentioned by the Bible is armed, and the first sword mentioned by the Bible—a flaming sword—is held by an angel. Yet for the last two hundred years arms and armed force have seemed to men's minds the work of the devil. Men aspired not to use and master this indispensable force for better ends, but to abolish it.

In 1784, after the end of the War of Independence, the majority of the Congress adopted the famous resolution: "Standing armies in time of peace are inconsistent with the principles of republican government, dangerous to the liberties of a free people and generally converted into destructive engines for establishing despotism." George Washington's army was reduced to seventy men. Fortunately for the U.S.A., this state of affairs did not last. But the spirit that inspired this resolution lived on.

With Wilson it blossomed again. "The new things in the world," he proclaimed less than two months before the beginning of the First World War, "are the things that are divorced from force." He believed in a mankind whose civilization would be preserved by its own power. Although the World War made him doubtful of this optimistic idea, he could not rid himself of his

2

aversion to armed force. The confused result of all this was a
League Covenant that treated the problem of problems, military
power, with a fatal vagueness and casualness, or, more accurately,
failed to treat it at all, but which nevertheless was credited with
the ability to transform history. The Covenant did not change
the military monopolies of the individual states in the least, nor
the lack of military power above them. It only recommended
that the states put their military forces at the disposal of the
League in an emergency—to lend them, as it were. This was only
a recommendation, it was not even juridically binding. There
was no compulsion to follow it. Despite the League, the military
basis remained unchanged, and the greatest undertaking of
progressivism, that of 1919, was nullified from the very outset
by its blindness to the importance of military power.

Fifteen years of attempts at "disarmament" followed. "Disarm!" cried the perfectionists—disarm the states without arming
any authority above the states. They believed sincerely that
gravitation was completely useless. And, incidentally, they failed
to understand that there simply was no such thing as disarmament. Even if not a single rifle, not a single cannon, not a single
bomb were left in the world, we should only be thrown back by
six hundred years—and then, too, battles were fought and people
were enslaved. Shovels and picks and pitchforks and kitchen
knives and even naked fists are just as sufficient to do evil—and,
after all, you cannot, by way of precaution, melt all the pitchforks and kitchen knives and chop off all fists. We cannot do
without armed force even against these—and we must make
that force as strong as possible. Equip it with good guns and
cannon!

No, we cannot dispense with gravity. We cannot turn up
our noses or stick our heads into the sand and escape the fact
of military power. No reforms float in the air, unanchored in
realities. Prolonged unity among a number of co-operating states
can only exist on a military basis.

Now, what prospect is there that the mammoth states, the
guardians, will renounce their armies, navies, and air fleets?
What prospect is there that they will merge their armed forces
into a common army, a common navy, a common air fleet, over
which no one of the participants would wield control? We know
that there is no prospect of this ever happening.

To be sure, a merger of the armed forces is not identical

with the merger of the states themselves. Such a merger we know would never be accepted. The conventional way to express this is to say that the states want to preserve their "sovereignty" and the note of deprecation with which many pronounce the term "sovereignty" is perhaps not quite justified. Be that as it may, in every respect except the military the states would remain entirely sovereign. They would be allowed to develop their own laws, institutions, economies, ideologies at will. By agreeing to amalgamate their armies they would give up only one component of their "sovereignty." But this one component represents ninety-five per cent of that same sovereignty. If anything in the world is certain it is that neither the Russians, nor the English, nor the Americans, nor the Chinese will agree to give up their individual armed forces and merge them into a common force.

They might accept something entirely different—an international police force. But at this point it is necessary to dispel a foggy notion that is popular. We will do well to realize clearly once and for all that an "international police force" is no solution of the great problem. In the form in which it is generally proposed it is only a secondary detail in a mechanism which in every other respect would remain unchanged. The national armed forces would not cease to exist; they would only lend a few of their regiments or divisions to this special force. The international police force would be stronger than the disarmed vanquished nations and possibly than some of the smaller powers; it would be weak and entirely useless with regard to the great powers. It would be a handy instrument for the great powers to use against others, but it would not in the least change the military situation among these mammoths themselves. There is the rub! We need not worry about how the mammoths will deal militarily with *the rest of the states*; what is important is with what military forces they will confront *each other*. The international police force will not create any new conditions for the guardians themselves; their behaviour will not be subjected to any new influences, and the harmony of their co-operation—which is the great problem— will not be strengthened. The international police force will offer a few modest technical advantages in cases where unity has existed before; but it will not be able to create and preserve unity. It will be a practical instrument, if the world council functions, but not an instrument that can make this council function. It would be well if this simple and far-reaching fact were kept more clearly in mind. Let us not pretend that the international police force can usher in a new historical era.

There can be no doubt about this: basically the military situation after the war will remain the same as it has always been. True, the military might of the council members will be un-challenged after victory. It will comprise almost four-fifths of the armed forces of the world. Wherever it is thrown in the balance, it will be irresistible. But it will not remain one cohesive force for good, definitively and irrevocably. Each of the mammoths will firmly retain its own force. Even such fascinating devices as Mr. Ely Culbertson's "world police" are impossible of realiza-tion, for ultimately this plan, too, would deprive every state of its own armed forces. No nation will ever accept such a plan. This is so certain that we can spare ourselves the trouble of deciding which solution we prefer; whether we like it or not, we cannot change the fact; no one can change it.

To be sure, in the realm of thought it is firmly established that we can achieve the domestication of the world only through the elimination of the military power of individual states and the creation of collective military power. This is as sure as sure can be in the realm of theory, and some day, in a hundred or a thousand years, it may come about. But not in the contemporary world, and there are even some weighty and legitimate reasons against its desirability. To be subjected without defence to every unpre-dictable majority resolution of an unpredictable council would be, in the world of to-day, a disquieting prospect for any nation —as disquieting for the United States as for the British Common-wealth or Soviet Russia or China. We should be in a difficult predicament if we had to decide whether we really want to deliver our country over to the definite compulsion of absolute, unconditional co-operation or whether we do not prefer to reserve some possibility of disagreement in extreme cases. This is a genuine dilemma.

And something else is perhaps even more depressing. The amalgamated armed force itself would have a disquieting aspect. Woe for us if this world-dominating machine ever fell into evil hands! Woe for us if its leaders should ever cease to be faithful servants of the world authority! With the turn of a hand they could impose a dictatorship upon the world against which there would be no conceivable resistance, and of which it would be more difficult to rid ourselves than of any previous dictator or conqueror.

Yes, there are dilemmas whose difficulty many manufacturers of perfect solutions seemingly have not even suspected. But, fortunately for our consciences, we are not asked to solve these dilemmas. They are purely theoretical and do not exist in the real world. For in the real world neither the governments nor the peoples of the three or four greatest powers will ever give up their own armed forces for any reason whatever.

We can agree that *unity of purpose among the members of the world authority could be relied upon only if they merged their individual armed forces into a collective superior armed force. And this will not come about.*

CHAPTER FIVE

THE LIMITS OF ALTRUISM

WE HAVE SEEN that we can have no assurance of the continued harmony of the members of the world council. This does not exclude the possibility that they may nevertheless remain in harmony; in many cases it may turn out that no fundamentally divergent interests will split them. Let us assume that there is agreement among them on the merits of a case which demands their intervention. Then comes the next stage of the problem: what will they actually do?

Let us suppose that the situation is a serious one. A powerful state, difficult to handle, has become aggressive toward one of its neighbours. It is true that immediately after this war only the guardians themselves will be really powerful; but the world does not stand still. Ten years after the next settlement there may be a state powerful enough to conjure up an international crisis. Nor can we reasonably exclude the possibility that in ten years a guardian state may become a menace to one of its neighbours. Let us suppose that all the mammoths of the world council except the offender agree on the matter. They see justice on one side and wrong on the other; they are unreservedly for right against wrong. But after this fortunate agreement on the merits of the case has been reached, there would still arise the question: what to do?

One thing must be made clear in advance: nothing will happen unless there exists a readiness to fight. The authority bent upon preventing or stopping a war must itself be ready to wage war. Armed force can be tamed only by armed force. To-day this may seem a well-worn truism, but between 1919 and 1939 it was not so; on the contrary, it was regarded as an expression of blood-thirsty, militaristic extremism. That period discovered a more comfortable solution of the problem. The twentieth century, it was maintained, can do without the old-fashioned bestiality of fighting. We can achieve the same result by streamlined, civilized methods—by "economic sanctions." The whole world cuts the delinquent nation off from imports, exports, credits, and communications, then comfortably looks on while the delinquent gradually and inevitably is strangled. That is how things are done in modern times!

This was one of the rosy illusions of an age which was rich in rosy illusions. The authors of this scenario overlooked the fact that there were two parties to this plot, not one. No one lets himself be strangled if he has a few muscles and a dagger; he stabs back. A resolute criminal will certainly stab back; he must be expected to do so. And if his opponents are not ready to parry expected stabs, they must abstain from trying to strangle him.

When the question of applying the much-vaunted "economic sanctions" arose for the first time, this obvious fact was at once revealed. This was in 1931. Japan pounced upon China. This was the occasion, if ever, for applying "economic sanctions." They would be particularly effective against Japan as she so largely depended upon imports. Moreover, in this case the United States, although not a member of the League, would participate in the action. But what if Japan did not submit? What if she attacked Indo-China, Malaya, Burma, the Philippines, the Dutch Indies, and Hong-Kong—all those places that have since become so familiar?

Briand and Sir John Simon asked each other whether they were ready to fight. And they answered each other: No! War must be avoided at all costs! They asked the Secretary of State in Washington the same question and Mr. Stimson answered: No! War must be avoided at all costs! At this point we need not discuss their reasons for this attitude; it is enough to note that they were not ready for the horrors and dislocations attendant upon a war, even a victorious war. And as they wanted to avoid war at all costs, "economic sanctions" were impossible. They were never adopted. For a year and a half an indecent game of camouflage and delay was carried on, and then the matter was dropped.

Was the lesson learned? Not in the least. In 1935–6, when Mussolini attacked Ethiopia, the clamour for "economic sanctions" was even stronger than in 1931. An unforgettable "peace ballot" held in England illustrated the state of mind that prevailed at that time. Many millions of voters, the majority of the country, in the same breath demanded economic sanctions and radical disarmament. The initiators of this ballot obviously did not suspect that there was even a remote connection between one's ability to strangle an adversary and one's ability to fight him. Once again the stratagem of "sanctions" was inseparably tied up with the danger of war—and possibly not with Italy alone, but also with Germany and Japan. But war was to be avoided at all costs—even a war that could be won. And so for the second time "economic sanctions" proved impossible. The notorious comedy of sham sanctions was staged to please those who favoured them and at the same time to avoid the risk of war. The export of goods that Italy could easily dispense with was stopped. The export of goods that were indispensable to Italy, such as oil, iron, and cotton, was permitted. Winston Churchill confirmed later that Mussolini himself specified which sanctions he would accept and to which he would reply by war. The limits he set were respected.

After this new fiasco the cult of "economic sanctions" began to wane. In the years that followed, while Hitler grew stronger and stronger, sanctions were vaunted less and less frequently as lightning in Jupiter's hands. But the ideology that gave rise to this invention is still alive. The liberalist aversion to military power is still latent. The superstition that economic factors are the most powerful force in the world is still rampant in all its variations. After this war the propensity to confuse the most comfortable solution with the most effective one may manifest itself with the same violence as after the last war. We must be for ever sceptical of all kinds of easy solutions. If the world authority is to be in a position to abolish wars, it must be ready to wage war: this is a *conditio sine qua non*. If this condition exists—and the other fellow always knows whether or not it does—even measures short of war may sometimes suffice. But without being backed up by this readiness to wage war, measures short of war are about as effective as prisons made of cardboard.

Now let us return to our problem. We left the members of the world council in the midst of a hypothetical crisis. We found them in heartening agreement on the merits of the case they had to cope with and wondered what they would actually do. Now we can make our question more specific: Would they brandish their weapons against the offender? Would they attack him if he attacked his victim?

The League of 1919 did not oblige them to do this. Many believe that the absence of such a pledge was at the root of the League's ineffectiveness. But the League Covenant did contain many a pledge that remained a dead letter. Hence we should not place too much trust in covenants. We have seen before that treaties among states usually contain the unwritten clause: "So long as it suits us." And we must add that not every breach of the treaty is an unmistakable act of dishonesty. Completely unequivocal treaties are rare, and there is always room for differences of interpretation. So let us not build on letters and paragraphs. What we are dealing with are states in full possession of their military power, and those who refuse to do their duty as guardians can hardly be compelled to do it. In the best case the member who deserts his duty could be penalized by the others. But punishing someone's refusal to fight is a different matter from forcing his participation in the fight. And even this punishment is conceivable only under the most exceptional circumstances. No, the text of covenants can give no certainty that the world council would adopt the resolution on which everything depends. Signatures are no guarantee that nations will be ready to risk their own blood in the defence of a threatened stranger. Such readiness is among the rarest things on earth. It could be called the fourth and highest degree of altruism.

The first degree and most common form of altruism is not to do evil to your fellow man. The second degree is to help your fellow man in overcoming the effects of evil he has suffered at another's hands. This form of altruism, which is less frequent than the first, involves positive action. The third degree is to help a fellow man resist the evil he is threatened with from another. The fourth degree of altruism is to go so far, in fighting for your fellow man, as to risk your own life, and possibly the lives of your family. Suppose we see a harmless passer-by in a deserted alley

attacked by men armed with revolvers. Will we attain the highest
degree of altruism by jumping to the defence of the victim? Will
we defy the guns and try to save the threatened passer-by at
the risk of our own life? Such things have happened. But more
often the opposite happens. Many have run away in such a case
and admitted freely that they refused to sacrifice their own lives
for the sake of a stranger. Others have declared: "I would have
acted differently if I had to think of myself only, but I have a
wife and children!" The propensity to run away in such cases
is obviously widespread.

It would be truly surprising if for once we found states nobler
than individuals. In fact history teaches us that in such cases
states run away even more frequently than do individuals. Cases
of nations taking up arms to save others from being raped are
extremely rare. Almost all world-conquerors have been successful
for the very reason that they were able to deal with their victims
one by one. We did not have to wait for Hitler to learn this:
it was also true of Xerxes, Alexander, Attila, Genghis Khan,
Omar, and Napoleon.

Is not this lack of altruism an essential characteristic of
states? Is not the very existence of different states equivalent to
a permanent declaration by each of them that it wants its fate
to remain separate from that of the others? Of course it is. If
the nations wanted to share their destinies, separate states would
be superfluous. By maintaining its separate existence each state
declares in effect: "As far as possible I do not wish to share the
difficulties of the others." This is the ultimate, entirely anti-
altruistic significance of the existence of separate states, and it is
no wonder that they have always acted accordingly. Occasionally
states have reached the lower degrees of altruism, but they have
almost never reached the highest. And if they did, if they really
helped another state by armed intervention, they were prompted
by interests of their own; egoism, not altruism, was the motive.

This is true, said the optimists of 1919. But, the tragedy
lies in the very fact that until now states have failed to understand what their really profound selfish interests required. To
save a threatened state is rarely simple altruism. It is always
egoism—a higher, maturer, more far-sighted egoism. For what
is at stake in such cases is not only the endangered state, but also
the international reign of law, which is advantageous to everyone. To defend the peace of any nation is to defend the peace

2*

of every nation. This must be realized, and now has been, after the unforgettable lesson of the war of 1914–18.

Thus the optimists of 1919 placed all their faith in the emergence of this far-sighted, sublimated egoism, which in effect was altruistic. They thought that a secular marriage of egoism and altruism had been consummated. Wilson was warned against this belief; he was told that he misinterpreted human nature, that human egoism was directed toward gaining immediate advantages and toward avoiding immediate disadvantages, that as a rule nothing else could be expected, and that after the infernal experience of the war that had just ended, egoism would desperately try to avoid a repetition. The President replied in a letter: "I feel the full weight of your fears. But it seems to me that the effects of this war may just as reasonably be expected to operate in the other direction." He did not hesitate to place his reliance on something of which he could say only that it "may just as reasonably be expected."

He was mistaken. During the two decades that followed, every aggression was in the last analysis treated as a threat to an individual foreign nation, not to the international reign of law. The sublime newfangled egoism with its slogan: "We must defend our own order against anarchy," was never victorious; the policies actually pursued were always inspired by the old primitive egoism. Not a single government or nation felt the Japanese invasion of Manchuria as an attempt against the common reign of law. In the last analysis, they felt that the matter concerned only China, and no nation wanted to make the supreme sacrifice for the sake of a foreign nation. This is how Mr. Stimson described the American raction to events: "To a great many of our people Manchuria was an unknown part of the world and they wondered what we had to do with any controversy there at all." And this was the reaction of the majority everywhere. Nowhere were the people willing to suffer and die for "the affairs of a foreign country of which we know little," as Neville Chamberlain said about Czechoslovakia. Against the assumptions of the optimists of 1919 this attitude was victorious in every country in the world without exception. It was not always victorious in all countries at the same time, but it was always victorious in a sufficiently large number to make any kind of collective action impossible. The will not to be entangled into making the highest sacrifices for the sake of a foreign nation's "affairs" was shared by the smallest and the greatest states alike. It dominated Belgium and Holland and Yugoslavia and Norway and Poland up to the very moment of their fall. It dominated France and England up to the moment of the German attack on Poland. It dominated Russia and the United States during the agonies of almost a dozen countries.

Are there any plausible reasons for expecting that in the future their reactions will be different? I do not know of any. The optimists of 1944 do not speak differently from those of 1919. They cite the need for the "reign of law," which they maintain is now realized more clearly than before. They adduce the higher, more far-sighted egoism of which, they think, people will now show themselves capable. But no one can explain why this should be true this time although it proved untrue the last time. The only reason given is that we have now gone through a harder school of experience than before, and that, as a result, the lesson must surely have been learned. But this school has been functioning since the dawn of time. The war of 1914 was not the first lesson but the thousandth, and the war of 1939 is not the second lesson, but the thousand and first. Each time the lesson was forgotten, and the difference between the thousandth and the thousand and first does not seem very weighty.

On the contrary, it might be argued that as a result of past experiences governments and nations have as a rule grown even more terrified of the prospect of war than they were before. We have seen how frantically they tried to avoid war, to defend not only allegedly foreign interests but even their own vital interests. Hitler's remilitarization of the Rhineland in 1936 was a murderous blow against the English, and even more particularly against the French. The two nations had long before concluded the Treaty of Locarno for the explicit purpose of preventing this blow. This treaty stipulated that they would reply to it by war, immediate war. But when the blow came they did not go to war. They dreaded war so much that they were not willing to wage it even on their own account. How can we expect them always to be willing to wage it for the sake of others in the future? It is not the worst characteristic of governments that they hesitate to sign the death sentence for countless thousands of brave people in Virginia and Idaho, or Essex and Yorkshire, in order to save other brave people in Shansi or Carinthia from disaster. Even though they are wrong theoretically, we can understand their scruples and excuses. At any rate, we must not expect that, from now on, such scruples and excuses will be absent. And it is quite certain that statesmen who hesitate to plunge their people into war will be supported by them. In all cases we have witnessed, the majority at least have supported them. Jones and Smith are honestly reluctant to die on behalf of Yuan and Petrovich.

These facts must be faced. It does no good to expect behaviour that conforms to cherished blueprints. What we should do, on the contrary, is to prepare blueprints adapted to behaviour which we have a right to expect. The quintessence of the world council is the readiness of its members to take up the cause of every threatened nation and, if necessary, to wage war on behalf of that nation. Upon this readiness the peace mission of the council stands or falls. We have examined a hypothetical case requiring the armed intervention of the world council and asked: What will it do? The answer to this question is unfortunately: we have no certainty that anything will be done at all. We cannot place any reliance on the willingness of the members to be always ready to wage war. They may be willing and they may not. Some may be willing, others not. And note that the desertion of one member would probably immobilize all the others. For even if only one of the big three decides to keep aloof, the others can hardly be expected to plunge into the cataclysm and spend themselves. The possibility that nothing will be done is a serious one.

We can agree that *the most important mission of the world authority can be fulfilled only if its members are willing to act in accordance with the highest altruism in every crisis. There is no certainty that they will do this.*

CHAPTER SIX

TWO COMPLETELY SEPARATE TASKS

WHERE DOES ALL this lead us? If there is no prospect of a new kind of military basis, no assurance of unity, no possibility of relying upon altruism, no certainty that a world authority would function, what then? Can we draw only negative conclusions from our analyses?

Not at all. Important positive conclusions can be drawn, but they are different from the usual clichés.

Let us go back to the great lesson of 1919. When the Peace Conference began, the establishment of the League of Nations was a foregone conclusion. For some strange reason Wilson and his friends had expected all sorts of sabotage of their project. But nothing of the kind occurred. There was no opposition to the idea of the League. The League was the very first question settled by the Paris gathering. Its founding required a shorter period in the many months of the conference sessions than any other important question: exactly eleven days. Rarely was a national law, and never was an international statute, enacted with less difficulty.

What was fought over for many months afterwards was something entirely different. Did the establishment of the League change the problem of the peace? Could a new kind of settlement be made because of the existence of the League? Or should a settlement of the old type be made because the effectiveness of the League was as yet uncertain? These questions created the conflict around the settlement of 1919. It was a conflict over the expediency of treating something that still had to be tested as something that had already been tested, a conflict over the extent to which the world authority could be relied upon.

In this conflict there were two parties, which might be called the doctrinaires and the empiricists, or the enthusiasts and the sceptics. The respective leaders of these two groups were Wilson and Clemenceau.

Wilson had certain new ideas for the settlement. He had developed them in his fourteen (or, more accurately, twenty-seven) points. These ideas were humane, liberalistic, idealistic. It was obvious that not many of them were in keeping with the world as it had always been. In that world few of the states, frontiers, and other solutions envisaged by the reformers of 1919, would have had any chance of survival. But fortunately, the reformers reasoned, the world would now be different. It would be a new world over which would float the all-powerful providence of the League smoothing out all conflicts, preventing all violence. Under the protection of this new giant, things were possible which had been inconceivable before.

Clemenceau thought otherwise. How could one speak of a giant, all-powerful? What had been created was only a newborn baby, and it had many weaknesses. For the time being, it was only an experiment which might easily end in failure. What then? What would happen to the states and frontiers and solutions, which admittedly had no solidity without a flourishing League? They would rot and wither away with the League— and this would mean that the fruits of victory would also rot and wither away, that all the sufferings and sacrifices had been in vain. For this reason the League and the settlement must be kept separate. The League must not be founded first and taken as the basis of a settlement which could not stand by its own strength. The exact opposite should be done: first the statesmen must make a settlement which could stand by itself, and then they should place the League above it and see what it could do.

The importance of this conflict cannot be exaggerated. Everything that followed was decided during this conflict.

Let us take the most important example: Germany. The problem was to prevent a German war of revenge. What Clemenceau demanded for this purpose was something that did not depend on the outcome of the experiment with a tentative world authority. He asked that the Rhineland be separated from the Reich forever, and that a Franco-British-American garrison be permanently stationed in this industrial province. If this proposal had been accepted, there would obviously have been no war to-day, and probably not even a Hitler. Germany would have had neither the courage nor the ability to sabotage the treaty for twenty years, or to rearm on a gigantic scale.

But in the eyes of the reformers of 1919 Clemenceau's proposals were hateful old-fashioned stuff. He violated all their principles and axioms. And they did not see what was his purpose; everything he wanted to achieve by these reprehensible methods, they thought would be achieved just as well and even better by the League. Why special guarantees in a world which enjoyed wholesale security through the League?

This was the decisive error. A rare and stubborn dogmatism prevailed among the reformers of 1919. They refused to see what was palpably clear. And they were stubborn not only with regard to the German problem. All the peace treaties contained provisions which were absolutely untenable if the League did not turn out to be the hoped-for giant. A number of states were created which would be simply suspended in air without the League. Innumerable details which were absolutely vital for

maintenance of normal relations among the states were settled
in such a manner that without the League a vacuum or a chaos
was bound to follow. It was, in truth, as Clemenceau put it,
"an unexampled misinterpretation and disregard of political
experience in the maelstrom of abstract thought."

The saddest part of all this was that there was no reason to
embark on such an extravagant gamble. For if the League
turned out to be a success, it would bring many blessings regardless of how the peace was written. The world over which the
League was to preside was the result of hundreds of very old-
fashioned treaties. No one thought of revamping the entire
planet. No one doubted that a successful League would be
beneficent even to the world as it was. Then why not add one
more settlement of the old type? Was not peace itself, which
would be guaranteed by the League, a sufficient blessing? More
than that, if the League was really to grow into a giant, could
it not later ennoble everything as much as it wanted? Those who
were most convinced that this world authority would be effective
could with the greatest confidence leave everything to its future
operation. It is important to realize that gambling in this matter
was either fatal or superfluous. It was fatal if the League did not
stand the test; it was superfluous if the League did stand the test.

Let us draw the lesson from all this. Once again we are approaching a similar situation. Here is the key to it. After this war
the urge to establish some sort of world authority will be hardly
less intense than after the last war. The will once more to attempt
it deserves as much encouragement as it did then. Although there
can be no certainty that it will succeed, there is no certainty
that it will fail, either. Even if it succeeds only partly or temporarily, it can be useful.

But we must see to it that the attempt does not degenerate
once again into a senseless gamble. Once again, after this victory
is achieved, the victors will hold a precious prize wrenched from
the jaws of hell. They must not again carry this prize directly
from hell to the roulette table and recklessly stake it on one
number called "world authority." They must not, in an effort
to increase the prize in this fashion, once again risk losing it at
one throw. Two completely separate tasks will confront the victors
after the last shot is fired; they must set out on their journey
to the future not on one rail but on two—one the rail of hope
and the other the rail of security. They should try to make the

world authority as much a reality as they can. But entirely independently of it a settlement must be made of which not one word, not one comma, not one regulation or mechanism presupposes the existence of a world authority. This settlement must be such that not one stone of it will be displaced even if the world authority becomes fragile. Let us proceed in such a way that we enjoy every possible benefit if the world authority stands the test, and suffer no loss if it does not. Let this be our guiding principle, our red thread leading us through the labyrinth of post-war problems.

Once the principle is accepted that the settlement should in no way depend upon the fate of the world authority, it will have to be a fairly robust, earthly kind of settlement. A number of intricate, subtle, risky novelties will have to be excluded; and this alone will simplify the problem.

But the problem of the world authority will be even more simplified. Once the principle is accepted that it cannot be, as Wilson put it, "the centre of the whole programme," but only an additional experiment, the whole perspective changes. The fact that its prospects are uncertain will no longer create insurmountable difficulties at every step. Nobody will need to feign certainty, which is not necessary in an experiment, and nobody will have to shrink from the uncertainties which are perfectly natural in an experiment. The results will show whether it is worth anything.

Take the problem of Soviet Russia, for instance. Without Russia the world council would be a cripple from the moment of its birth. But it is also true that the future role of Russia is more problematical than that of any other power. It is a fact that for twenty-three years almost everywhere in the world Russia pursued a policy the aims of which were antagonistic to those of her present allies. We are told that she will never pursue such a policy again. Perhaps she will not. But assurances and gestures made during a war have never yet been regarded as gilt-edged securities. The question is whether Russia will not use her membership some day to make the council a failure rather than a success. This question is historically so legitimate that it cannot be removed from the minds of responsible statesmen. And there is no way of avoiding it as long as the world council is conceived as the "centre of the whole programme." It will be almost impossible to harmonize the following three things: a council whose failure would result in a general catastrophe; a council whose failure could be caused by any of its members; and a council one of whose members will be suspected of deliberately wishing its failure. I submit that in this case the uncertainty over Russia's future policy will prove an insurmountable obstacle. But this uncertainty will be as acceptable as any other if the whole undertaking is conceived of only as an additional experiment.

Take another example: the question of form and organization. They are almost impossibly difficult if the whole peace settlement is to be based on the world council. In this case the perfection of the council's statutes would be decisive, and all those questions of form, organization, procedure, which I have elsewhere called secondary, would become overwhelming. All of them have their importance and interest, but they recede to their rightful secondary place if the enterprise is frankly and resolutely conceived of as an experiment. For what is to be tested is the will, not the forms. Let us imagine the simplest form conceivable for the world authority—a statute containing only one sentence: "The contracting parties pledge themselves to assist every threatened or attacked state by all the means at their disposal, including military force." If the will expressed in these words persists, even this elementary form will provide the machinery through which everything that is required can be done. If not, even the most ingenious document will not prevent the powers from failing to do what is required. I am not advocating the choice of this elementary form; I only want to illustrate to what extent questions of form retreat into the background if we conceive of the world authority as an experiment—an experiment the outcome of which does not depend on forms, but on the will behind it.

Yes, the will is the decisive factor—the will alone, the will that we cannot estimate as yet and can influence only very little, the will of many countries, not only of our own—and their will not only on the morrow of victory, but also in the years that follow. Our influence on the treaties and institutions the members of the world council will be ready to accept after victory will be small enough; not even our voice penetrates countries like China or Russia. Our influence to-day on the will of the future is even smaller. What the old Dane, Helmuth von Moltke, the only great general the Germans had in the last century, said of war applies also to the world authority: "You can control the mobilization, but after the first shot is fired you sail out into a completely unknown sea."

In matters pertaining to the world authority one sails out into a completely uncharted sea. The voyage must be undertaken, for mankind demands it, and our remorse would become an unbearable torment if it were not undertaken. But the sea is uncharted. The calculable forecasts are not valid very far out. We may encounter shores of which we know nothing to-day. If the council does not function forever it may function for a few years, and this alone may be extremely beneficial. It may preserve itself by the admission of new members or the replacement of old ones. Even if it retrogresses, it may not dissolve into nothingness; it may leave behind it alliances and friendships, just as the Holy Alliance left behind it a loose organism, called the "European Concert," which was not the worst thing in the world. The world council may leave behind it a loose "world concert." Life is "perpetual creation." The favourable opportunities that may present themselves in the course of the voyage are incalculable and infinite. And if we rigorously eliminate all improper risks from the experiment, we may look forward to these opportunities with a tempered optimism.

We can agree that *the world authority is an experiment which must be undertaken but which may fail. A peace settlement must be made which can survive even if this experiment fails.*

Part Three: Anti-War Panaceas

CHAPTER SEVEN

THE ECONOMIC ILLUSION

LET US LEAVE the world authority and take up the question of the settlement that can endure by its own strength. How can such a settlement be made? Is there a serum against war?

This sounds somewhat farcical, but it is less farcical than it seems. Since natural science set out on its triumphant march, the faith that problems relating to human society can also be solved with exactitude has been ineradicable. For instance, war: is it not a disease of the international organism? If so, it must be possible to discover its cause and a remedy for it.

A few "scientific" theories on the causes of war have become popular with everyone from village schoolmasters to university professors. The most popular of them is beyond doubt the economic theory, according to which wars originate in economic causes and can be prevented by economic means.

This theory is obviously an offshoot of the tree planted about a hundred years ago by the two founders of the socialist church. Karl Marx and Friedrich Engels proclaimed that everything in human history arises from economic causes. This was their famous "materialist conception of history." It became, quite understandably, one of the greatest intellectual hits of all times. This doctrine has a magnetic effect on the two strongest tendencies of the human intellect: one is the most modern of its tendencies, and the other the oldest.

The "materialist conception of history" presented itself as an exact science. That was its modern appeal. According to the fathers of socialism, it was so exact and scientific that through it the whole future of mankind could be determined in advance, "like a process of natural history." Economic facts produce history "with the inexorability of a law of nature." But in addition to this modern scientific appeal, the dogma also has the oldest appeal: that of being a total explanation. The most primitive, most immortal aspiration of the human mind is to have one explanation for all the confusingly diverse phenomena in the world, an explanation that is valid for everything. This demand for complete explanations created the gods. It set a thousand philosophers into motion, from the first, Thales of Miletus, who explained the universe as a product of water, to our contemporary, Henri Bergson, who interpreted all human activity as the product of the *élan vital*. The same tendency presents us from time to time with medical fads according to which all diseases stem from microbes or hormonal disturbances or blood infections. This tendency makes it possible to convince people time and again that the source of all their mishaps is the heretics or the witches or the Jews or some other supposedly universal power of evil. The economic interpretation of history was marvellously adapted to satisfying both the oldest and the most modern intellectual demands: it gave to the former a comforting complete explanation and to the latter an awe-inspiring quantity of seemingly exact scientific data. Thus it irresistibly swept over the world.

Tested by the facts of many decades, it proved to be a colossal chimera. The facts stubbornly refused to conform to the dogma. But this did not prevent the kernel of that dogma from taking solid root in the brains of half of mankind. It implanted itself almost as firmly in the minds of anti-socialists as in those of the socialists. If the kernel of Marxism is the belief that the fate of mankind is determined by economics, the millionaires, bankers, industrialists, and Tory politicians of our century are hardly less Marxist than the paupers, professional revolutionists, radical journalists and novelists. America, which thinks that she is fairly free of Marxism, is hardly less Marxist than the European countries in which the doctrine flourished. In particular, it has hardly been possible to dispute the theory that war stems from economic causes, and even to-day it is not easy. Popular belief in this theory displays a variety of nuances. The most primitive, and therefore the most widespread, can be described as follows: Wars arise from economic distress. The "have-nots" rebel against the "haves." To use a metaphor, the beast becomes aggressive when it is hungry. Such is the idea which seems to dominate the minds of to-day's most popular world reformers.

If this idea were true, there really would be a serum against war. A permanent settlement would be one which removes the economic plagues of the nations. All the economic desiderata of the countries involved would be tabulated; each would announce what amount of foodstuffs, raw materials, machines, and so on, per head and per year, would be sufficient to satisfy her. The question would be settled by way of a general collective bargaining. All nations would be given "freedom from want." All would be satisfied and peace would be secured. But this idea is refuted by hundreds of concrete facts and theoretical considerations. And one of these facts is strong enough to demolish not only the economic theory of war but also the entire "materialist conception of history"—the indisputable fact that it is men who act, not economic conditions. Everything derives from the will or emotions of people. If economic facts produce any political results, it is only through the detour of a transformer station, the transformer station of the human mind or emotions. But who can foretell how an economic fact will transform the human will or heart?

The tragedy or comedy of all the nuances of the economic interpretation of history begins right here. The erudite and the naïve devotees of this interpretation take it for granted that the same economic cause will always and everywhere produce the same effects in the psyche of the persons concerned. According to them, economic distress, for instance, always makes people wild, and prosperity always makes them gentle. But not a whit of this is true! The human soul is much more irregular and incalculable than that. Economic distress, for instance, does not necessarily make people wild. It can just as well make them more cautious. And economic prosperity does not necessarily make people gentler; it can just as easily make them more aggressive.

The professional revolutionists, for instance, who are sworn historical economists, were always absolutely certain that a deteriorating economic situation would make the workers more revolutionary. To their bewilderment, often—even most of the time—exactly the reverse took place. The German Socialist workers were most radical, most conscious of their strength, in a period of prosperity. Their greatest electoral success occurred in 1928. But when depression and unemployment set in, they did not grow more revolutionary, they grew more humble. Fear of losing even the job they still had made them increasingly more submissive, inert, and fatalistic. A similar development took place in England. The Labour Party reached its peak at the peak of prosperity in 1929. When depression and economic distress set in, they gave rise not to more radicalism, but to more conservatism. Is it different in the international field? A great many wars in modern times have been undertaken by nations who enjoyed the highest degree of abundance. And on the other hand nations suffering from the worst economic distress have not undertaken wars. The economaniacs have a hard time explaining the wildness of the sated beast and the gentleness of the hungry one.

No, there is not the shadow of a rule which prescribes how economic facts will affect the human will and emotions and thereby influence the course of political events. Their effects are irrational and unpredictable. I have said that this is the most fundamental refutation of the economic interpretation of history and, as a result, of the alleged economic cause and cure of war.

It is not the only one.

How do wars really arise? One cannot help mentioning at least briefly that as a rule wars are brought about by a few people. They, not the entire nation, decide to wage war. This is relevant for us because it shows that wars are not necessarily caused by concern for national interests, economic or extra-economic. Very often, as we know, the motives of these gentlemen have been purely personal. They wanted to distinguish themselves; to show what they could do; to appear as great men before their contemporaries and posterity. Or they wanted to give their control a firmer basis by brilliant military triumphs, or to silence rivals and opponents, or to overcome difficulties of one kind or other.

But, of course not all wars are unleashed for purely personal motives. And even when they are, the responsible gentlemen usually convince themselves that their own interests and the best interests of their nation are identical. Even the most cynical warmongers, from Nebuchadnezzar to Hitler, can be credited with believing that they served the interests of their nation. Now, what advantage does a nation extract from a victorious war? What is the advantage for the sake of which cynics or noncynics undertake wars? This advantage is usually something more important than any economic profit. It is power! The object of every war is power, an effort to increase it or prevent it from decreasing. And a gain in power is far more than an economic gain, just as the whole is far more than the part.

True, that great thing called power also contains an economic ingredient. But this is only one among many other ingredients. For instance, military force, too, is an ingredient of power: the possession of armies and weapons and strategic territories, and the superiority of one's own potential over others' potentials. Spiritual power, too, is an ingredient of power: the influence on minds within and beyond one's own territory, and the ability to triumph over competing influences. All these various components put together result in power pure and simple. And it is not even true, as many believe, that the economic ingredient is the most important in this complex. By no means. Each of these ingredients can to a certain extent replace any of the others. We see that the Vatican has a considerable regular income as a result of its influence on people's minds; here the spiritual ingredient produces economic results. We have seen countries collapse in wars at least partly because propaganda had paralysed their strength; here the spiritual ingredient produced military results. But although any component of power can under certain circumstances function as a substitute for any other, by far the strongest among them is certainly the military component, not the economic. It can most extensively replace the others and it is most irresistible in bringing the others into line. Just as a revolver in the hand of the hold-up man suffices to wrench hundreds of thousands of dollars from the millionaire, so the power of arms enables the conqueror to seize all the economic resources of entire countries. Hitler has shown this, first in Germany and later in all the countries he subjected. Blanqui, a heretic French Socialist, coined the formula: "*He who has steel has bread.*" Significantly enough, when Mussolini left the Socialist Party in 1914 and founded his own newspaper, he put this formula as a motto on its masthead.

Increase of power in all its aspects is the fruit of a victorious war. Increase of power pure and simple, as a whole, is the motive for which wars are undertaken. Its purely economic profit is usually not in a rational relation to the sacrifices, costs, and risks of a war; particularly not in modern times. But the profit in power as a whole: that is something different. It is much more and much more often worth the sacrifices and risks involved.

This does not preclude the possibility that now and then an economic objective has been particularly attractive among the gains in power envisaged. "If we conquer, we gain great new power, part of which will be such and such a coal mine, factory or grain-producing territory"—in this sense it is certainly conceivable that the economic motive sometimes plays an important part, occasionally even a preponderant part, in unleashing a

war. But history offers few such examples. Of no great war of
the last century can it be seriously said that in the power motive
which unleashed it the economic component was predominant.

Bismarck waged his wars in order to merge the separate
German states into one single state under Prussia's leadership—
a typical power motive. All the conceivable subdivisions of
power were of course included. But if one of the subdivisions
was predominant, it was the military rather than the economic.
Nor can any dominant economic motive be discovered in the
outbreak of the war of 1914. Those who tried for two decades
in the sweat of their brows to find such a motive lost themselves in the most absurd fantasies, paralogisms, and sophisms.
In fact all sorts of motives were present: the preservation of Austria-
Hungary, the expansion and military strengthening of Germany,
the separation and defeat of inconvenient neighbours. Such a
gigantic power-political programme necessarily contained all
kinds of benefits for the economic ingredient of power as well.
But that these by-products played a causative part in producing
the war is pure fiction.

Least of all is it true of Hitler that he began his war as a poor
"have-not" against the rich "haves." He quite certainly was
not guided by economic but by far more extensive desires. In
the first place, Germany, despite all the propagandist clamour
on this subject, was not a "have-not"—it was on the contrary
one of the very big "haves"; it had no real economic troubles.
In the second place, what could be represented as such had been
produced artificially by war preparations: "guns instead of
butter." And in the third place, Hitler again and again had the
opportunity to give up war in return for the fattest sort of
economic compensation—and he chose otherwise: he chose war.
He chose it purely and simply for the sake of power. And in his
version of power everything is reduced to the military component.
Mein Kampf culminates in a manifesto which Hitler calls "The
Political Testament Forever of the German Nation Concerning
Its Activity with Regard to the Outside World." It recommends
that Germany do not permit any other state with military power
or even potential military power to exist or arise beside her.
Germany has "not only the right, but the duty to prevent by all
means, including the use of the force of arms, the coming into
existence of such a state, or if such a one has already come into
existence, to demolish it." There is not a word about economics.

Let us give up the popular notion that wars arise from economic causes. And let us also give up the notion that there is an economic serum against war.

Supposing that wars are provoked by economic motives, it must still be granted that economic motives cannot be eradicated. After what you call distress has disappeared, the nation does not cease to have economic wishes and appetites. The have-not who has become the have becomes the have-not-enough. The grievance of to-day is followed by the greed of to-morrow. In so far as economic motives are dangerous for the peace, greed is just as dangerous as grievances.

But, above all, the economic motives are not the real causes of war. Wars are undertaken to increase or preserve power—great power in the case of the great nations and little power in the case of the little. In the complex of power the economic motives are only a small part. Even if it were possible to make this small part harmless effectively and permanently—and this is impossible—the other more dangerous components would still remain. There is no chance of banishing the dangers of the urge for power by some sort of economic transaction. When the "will to power" becomes virulent, all the economic serums fails.

We must be clear about this if only to gain a negative knowledge: the knowledge of what is impossible. Economic projects are multiplying. They are vaunted as projects which will produce not only well-being and wealth, but also peace via well-being and wealth. Our experiences with a settlement which relies on such miracles will be bitterly disappointing. International planning boards and world investment boards may be constituted; every reasonable method of multiplying trade may be applied; possibly even that phrase which is thus far completely empty, "free access to raw materials," may some day be given some concrete substance. A high degree of prosperity in all the countries of the world may thus be achieved. All this will be highly welcome. But it will not bury the will to power under a hedge of roses and prevent that will from stirring.

The idea that well-being tames the urge to power and eliminates the inducement to acts of violence is beautiful, but deceptive. Look at Germany: whence her second World War? Is it an explosion due to economic misery and despair, as we are asked to believe? Then how could we explain her first, the Wilhelminian World War? At that time the country was indisputably swimming in wealth. As producer, earner, international creditor, she had moved into the second place, right behind England, by leaps and bounds. She had only to keep quiet in order to move into the first place in less than five years. But she started a war. She made war when she was rich. She made war when she was—allegedly— poor.

We can agree that *wars are undertaken for power motives. Economic measures offer no prospect of pacifying the urge for power and securing peace.*

CHAPTER EIGHT

THE SECRETS OF ELDERS OF FINANZION

THERE IS ANOTHER economic interpretation of war, according to which it is caused not by the economic greed of the nations, but by that of a small group within each nation. Capitalism, or the capitalists, cause wars. There will be wars as long as they exist, and to get rid of wars one must throw out capitalism and the capitalists.

For a quarter of a century this idea has been spread throughout the world. After the birth of the Soviet state, in 1917, it was sent out into the world with a stormy dynamism. The impression made by it was so profound and so vast that its origin and context were soon practically forgotten. It struck roots in millions who in other matters neither were nor are socialists, neither know nor want to know anything of any doctrine whatsoever. The dogma freed itself from its origins. We experienced that memorable investigation in Washington, during which resolutely anti-socialist senators made a strenuous effort to unmask the responsibility of Morgan and other millionaires for America's entry into the World War. Apparently Senator Nye was not even clearly aware of the fact that he was only adopting the favourite gospel of Lenin. The belief that all wars must stem from the capitalists of all countries without distinction had gone beyond the rational stage—it had entered the realm of folklore.

It still is a part of folklore even though during the present World War we see fairly few public manifestations of it. In the Allied countries, if the subject is touched upon at all, only the

Axis capitalists are blamed. They ordered their servant Hitler to start the war. But even this accusation, if it were true, would reflect on the entire capitalist system. The implication would remain that capitalists are always behind such crimes. And in fact even to-day the idea is latent in men's minds. As soon as the settlement has to be made, we shall once again hear stormy predications that peace can be secured by more socialism.

But are wars really caused by capitalism? It would be very good if they really were. Then we would have the panacea. Then we could sharpen our knives with enthusiasm, preparing for the great operation. But is it really so? What is the text of the indictment?

The socialist theory of war is fortunately exact and well elaborated. It explains in detail how the capitalists produce wars and why they cannot help producing them. Let us glance at it.

We must mention that to speak of "the" socialist theory of war is inaccurate; for there are at least two such theories: a new one and an old. And the new is the opposite of the old, Lenin's is the opposite of Marx's.

In 1848, when Marx and Engels hurled their *Communist Manifesto* at mankind, the bourgeois-individualistic economic system which they baptized by the more hostile name of "capitalism" was still young. Only fifty years earlier it had followed the decrepit system of state intervention known as mercantilism, which had in the end been hated like the pest. Marx and Engels had no love for the young system that succeeded mercantilism. But when they examined the world, they noticed that since the victory of capitalism no more wars had occurred. The rumble of cannon had not been heard since the fall of Napoleon in 1815, and, on the whole, peace reigned. This was a fact. From this fact the two founding fathers distilled a scientific "law": they deduced that capitalism was a peaceful force. In their *Manifesto*, which unfolded the future of mankind, they wrote: "National differences and antagonisms between peoples are daily vanishing more and more owing to the development of the bourgeoisie. . . ."

It goes without saying that this was not meant as a declaration of love for the bourgeoisie. The purpose pursued by the bourgeoisie was still exploitation of the workers. But, thanks to the capitalist system, Marx and Engels thought, the bourgeois of the dominant nations no longer needed to carry on exploitation on a competitive basis; they could do it on a co-operative basis.

They extended fraternal hands over the frontiers. They associated in all kinds of international cartels, syndicates, and pools. An international family of vampires ever more systematically sucked out the blood of their own peoples and peoples at a lower stage of development. But all this took place without wars, within the family. Although repellent in every other respect, capitalism furthered peace among the leading capitalist nations.

Such was the original socialist doctrine concerning the relations between war and capitalism. It excellently fitted the facts so long as these facts remained as Marx and Engels had found them. But soon after the publication of the *Communist Manifesto* isolated wars began again here and there. Events moved away from the theory, and for a few decades the theoreticians tried to find a way out of the dilemma with interpretations and complementary theories. Finally came 1914 and the greatest war ever seen. It was a war between the leading capitalist states. One of the many consequences of this tragedy was the birth of a new socialist doctrine of war. A man in Switzerland whose name was Lenin relegated the old Marxian science of the pacific effects of capitalism to the junk pile, once and for all. In his book *Imperialism, the Final Stage of Capitalism* he showed in detail how the war of 1914 had been born out of capitalism, and how it could not have been otherwise; and how from then on the same thing would necessarily happen again. This book of Lenin's is the modern socialist theory of war. It is canonized. Those who do not know it surely know the formula "imperialist war," which is the epitome and label of the doctrine.

What, then, does this doctrine teach? At its basis is a premise which is fundamental to every variety of Marxism. It is the idea that in every capitalist country the legal political authorities are figureheads. The real rulers are the capitalists, and all government organs must obey them. In any capitalist country—on this point the socialist dogma is clear and firm—the authorities must dance to the tune played by the capitalists. They only carry out orders; they are "lackeys," as Lenin put it. When the capitalists give orders, presidents, cabinets, parliaments, dictators, czars, and kaisers must carry them out, whether they will or not.

For what reason must they carry them out? Why, indeed? The reason cannot be seen with the naked eye. To the naked eye, even the dictators do not seem to be the servants of the capitalists —rather the reverse seems to be the case. Who has the power of

deposing, arresting, or shooting the other fellow? The dictator
rather than the capitalists. And in democracies the presidents,
ministers, and parliaments seem to be put in office and directed
by a conglomeration of highly diversified, divergent, and often
changing wills. Many democratic governments seem not only
not to obey the capitalists but also to treat them for years at a
stretch in a way which makes them furious. In brief, the capitalists
seem to be only one of the many sources of influence; a source
which is sometimes very powerful, sometimes very weak, but never
even remotely the only source. Why, then, is this appearance
only a delusion? The reason is not given. In the classic works
of modern socialism you will find it said a hundred times that
all this is only a delusion; a hundred times it is hammered into
you that secretly, subterraneously, the capitalists, despite all
appearances to the contrary, dominate the governments. But
why this is so and cannot be otherwise is not demonstrated. It
must be believed. It is one of the many mythological elements
that are abundantly present in the socialist science. The premise
of the socialist doctrine of war is: if the capitalists want war the
governments must wage it.

But why do the capitalists want war? Why should the capitalist
system inevitably beget the capitalists' need for war?

Lenin explains this by the fact that the capitalist system has
entered into a stage of sclerotic old age. In its "early stage," as
Marx has shown, this system caused national antagonisms to
vanish. But since capitalism entered its final stage, this truth
has turned into its opposite: "Capitalism, formerly a liberator
of nations, has now, in its imperialist stage, become the greatest
oppressor of nations. . . . Humanity must now for years, nay,
decades, witness armed conflicts of the 'great' nations for an
artificial maintenance of capitalism."

What exactly does take place in the "final stage"? In this
stage capitalism finds itself in a situation which it has not known
until then. It becomes more and more apparent that opportunities
for increasing profits on the home market are as good as exhausted.
The number and size of the enterprises can no longer be sub-
stantially expanded. The capitalists accumulate profits from old
enterprises, but they find it hard to invest them lucratively in
new enterprises. Thus a new thing arises in the annals of mankind:
liquid capital—"finance capital"—for which there are no more
pasture grounds, so to speak, in its own country. But at the same

time something else unfortunately takes place. Until then the dominant element in the capitalist camp has been relatively satisfied industrial capital. For some reason finance capital now becomes dominant. Thus we find ever hungrier and greedier—and also more powerful—finance capitalists! The drama begins to take shape.

It unfolds according to inexorable laws. The finance capitalists are compelled to cast their eyes beyond the frontiers of their own countries. They must discover foreign countries where their hungry capital can still find rich pasture lands. What they discover are the backward, undeveloped, colonial, or semi-colonial countries. Africa, and the Balkans and South America still need capital. There profits can still be made. And so the finance capitalists begin to "export capital" into the backward countries. But here, too, the opportunities are not unlimited. And, most important, these opportunities are not discovered by the finance capitalists of one single country. French, German, and English finance capitalists try to export capital simultaneously into the same backward countries (in 1914 America did not yet export capital). And so they encroach upon one another—and not only as individuals. Rivalry arises not only among the individual finance capitalists but also among capitalist groups. And as they are now fighting for their last remaining opportunity to make profits, their competition must inevitably become more and more bitter. More and more desperate grow their efforts to outplay and dislodge one another. The drama now rushes toward its climax.

This climax is reached when the finance capitalists get so mad at each other that capital export to the backward countries becomes a real inferno, which in addition is unprofitable. From that point on, the means of economic competition fail, and inescapably the finance capitalists are transformed into financial imperialists. As they have become the dominant category of capitalists and their governments have become their personal lackeys, they command their respective governments to rid them of their intolerable competitors by military force. The French, for instance, may give orders that Morocco be incorporated into the French Empire, in order that their competitors be prevented from entering Morocco. Even this may be sufficient to produce a colossal war. But the orders may be even more extreme. For instance, the German finance capitalists order their government to subject England to the German Empire, and the British finance capitalists issue a similar order to their government, in order to get rid of their chief competitor. This is their last resource in order to preserve the last source of profit that remains open to them. Unavoidably they make use of this last resource. And the government obeys. A crisis is contrived, and the "imperialist war" is here. Thus it came about in 1914, and thus it must inevitably come about again and again during the "final stage" of capitalism. Such is the exact doctrine from which the folklore has developed.

Disappointingly enough, it does not stand up at any point. We are confronted with the exceptional case of a construction in which not a single one of the facts asserted has any relation to the true facts and in which not a single one of the logical connections and inferences has any resemblance to logic. The whole theory was absurd even with regard to the war of 1914. It is even more absurd with regard to the war of 1939.

The very starting-point of the theory is absolutely unacceptable. Wars have existed in all the past centuries. The drive for creating and expanding empires has existed under every economic system. What a violation of logic suddenly to make capitalism— its "final stage," indeed—responsible for war! And the conclusion is as logical as the starting-point. Why must the competition among capitalists unavoidably be decided by guns? Why should the same gentlemen who iron out all their other conflicts so well through the mechanism of pools, cartels, and societies be incapable of doing the same thing when it comes to capital export? The vital element in business is compromise. By what logic can one impute to business men the mentality of people running amuck on one single subject?

No less fantastic than the logic were the "facts" on which this doctrine was based, even the "facts" before 1914. It was a fantasy that the finance capitalists had ever been different from the industrial capitalists; they were for the most part the same gentlemen. It was a fantasy that finance capital was the dominant element in capitalism. In so far as a vague distinction between the two categories was possible, industrial capital was definitely dominant in many countries, particularly in Germany. It was a fantasy that finance capital had no other possibility for profitable investment than the backward countries. Less than twenty per cent of capital investment went to such countries year after year;

and about eighty per cent went to the home market and other highly developed countries. It was a fantasy that competition in capital exports was particularly keen. In fact it was less sharp than in the export of goods. Moreover, national predilections had been formed. French capital export preferred Russia; German preferred America; British, the Empire and Asia. The various capitalists encroached upon one another relatively little.

As for the order to wage war which the finance capitalists allegedly issued, well, this theory was transformed into one of those ironies with which history sometimes surprises us. For if there was in 1914 one great power of finance capital, it was the so-called City of London. This was the head and the heart and the biceps of all world financial power. Now, it is a historical fact that the City of London made efforts to the very last moment to prevent its government from entering the war of 1914—most wrongly so and most unsuccessfully so. One of its many moves in this direction is mentioned, for instance, by Lloyd George in his memoirs: "On Saturday [August 1, 1914] the Governor of the Bank of England called on me, as Chancellor of the Exchequer, to inform me on behalf of the City that the financial and trading interests in the City of London were totally opposed to our intervening in the war." And with a few picturesque strokes of the brush he depicts how the finance capitalists—the real living ones, not the imaginary ones—actually behaved in those days: "There are those who pretend to believe that this was a war intrigued and organized and dictated by financiers for their own purpose. . . . I was Chancellor of the Exchequer and, as such, I saw money before the war; I saw it immediately after the outbreak of the war; I lived with it for days and did my best to steady its nerve, for I knew how much depended on restoring its confidence; and I say that money was a frightened and trembling thing: money shivered at the prospect. It is a foolish and ignorant libel to call this a financiers' war."

And finally, how about our own time, this present war, to-day's "final stage"? We have heard the slogan about "the imperialist war" repeated as noisily as ever; but what a pitiful pauper it has become in the interval! In fact, the thing that is supposed fatally to beget war in the final stage of capitalism did not even exist in 1939! In 1914 capital export to backward countries existed; there was at least some competition in this

business. In 1939 both the business and the competition were
absent. For the preceding ten years finance capitalism had
definitely ceased to be a migrant bird and had become rather
like an oyster. Whatever may have been the source of the finance
capitalists' profits, it certainly was not capital export, the allegedly
last source. Since 1930 there has been practically no export of
capital. Actually it was legally forbidden in almost all countries.
The very thing which according to Lenin's "law" produces
wars in the final stage had simply vanished from the world.
The whole basis of his construction had gone to pieces.

And this was not all! The doctrine which had become a
theoretical ghost was now made a laughing-stock in practice.
Between 1935 and 1938 the accusation that the finance capitalists
caused the "imperialist war" on behalf of their private interests
was replaced by the opposite accusation. Everything was turned
upside down. The finance capitalists were suddenly those who
"appeased" on behalf of their private interests. In September
1939 this theory was again turned upside down. Now again the
war was suddenly the result of a plot by the finance capitalists:
it was an "imperialist war." And after June 22, 1941 there was
still another reversal. The finance capitalists and the imperialist
war were dropped, and the war became a war of the "freedom-
loving peoples."

Thus it went, one way or another. If ever a dogma has
been debased by its own church, it is this one. It is difficult to
judge whether Lenin himself took his theory seriously; whether
even he did not intend it only as propaganda—extremely effective
propaganda—in scientific disguise. At any rate what still survives
of this theory to-day lives exclusively on its propaganda appeal.
It is the same sort of propaganda appeal of which the Nazis took
advantage in the famous *Protocols of the Elders of Zion*. The kinship between the two is striking. In Lenin's theory also a devilish
occult power was represented as dwelling deeply hidden in the
mechanism of history. According to him, also, this occult power
is driven by demoniac profit motives and possesses overwhelming strength. I submit that the Elders of Zion and the giants of
Finanzion are members of the same mythological family. They
belong to the tribe of those superhuman, omnipotent, irrational,
and invisible powers which produce evil in the world. They both
are examples of those anthropomorphic universal explanations
of evil for which mankind from its beginnings until to-day has

3

always asked and which have again and again been given i under all possible names and disguises.

Only in the realm of this mythology does the hope subsis that war can be abolished by the abolition of capitalism. In the realm of reality many capitalists in many cases have been fo: war—without being the decisive factor in producing it. Bu even more capitalists have been more frequently against war, fo appeasement—without being the decisive factor in that, either For someone who owns more, and therefore risks more, to be against war is the normal reaction. Particularly in modern time: the risks involved in war have grown so enormously that the larger number of capitalists have almost always been "frightened and trembling," advising and urging appeasement. Sometime this advice was useful, sometimes immensely harmful for the world. And real developments have not in the least confirmed the theory that the liquidation of capitalism liquidates war. I my memory does not deceive me, the only existing state withou capitalism and capitalists has recently invaded no less than si countries; and if these invasions did not lead to war in each case, it was due only to the fact that resistance was not alway offered. Of course, of course, there were reasons for invading these countries. They were indispensable strategic bases; they had formerly belonged to Russia; and brothers of Russian blood lived there. But hundreds upon hundreds of other wars have been waged for the same reasons. These are the traditiona reasons.

We can agree that *war is not a product of capitalism. The abolition of capitalism will not guarantee peace.*

CHAPTER NINE

THE SEDUCTION OF CHEMISTRY

ONE OF THE most troublesome characteristics of this world is its lack of uniformity. Geographically it is "one world." It is one because everything that happens anywhere can have consequences everywhere. But in many other highly important respects the world is definitely not one. One must live in many countries for many years to understand how many worlds there are.

At first sight these countries seem to be, let us say, ninety-five per cent identical. Various languages are spoken, but each can be translated into the others. Certain foods are prepared differently here and there, the houses are a little higher or lower, the customs vary—but all this seems secondary. Everywhere the people practise the same pursuits, have approximately the same institutions, tools, and goods, mostly the same God; and they always are born and die in the same way.

But slowly, very slowly, differences reveal themselves—differences to a degree which one would barely believe possible within the framework of all the external similarities. The nations think differently and feel differently. What one considers agreeable, another considers hateful. What is a matter of complete indifference to one is for another an object of violent attraction or aversion. They react to the same stimuli in completely unlike ways, and the same reactions manifest themselves in completely unlike behaviour. Thousands of years have developed the most astonishing incompatibilities under a superficial identity. Many worlds! What is valid in one of these worlds is not necessarily valid in the others. What is positive in one can be completely negative in the others.

When the settlement is written, it will have to deal with many worlds. We are lacking, as we have seen, not only one great universal panacea for war. Even partial recipes applicable everywhere have not thus far been discovered. It is fairly certain that every individual can be put to sleep with a certain dose of morphine, and that a certain dose of caffein will accelerate every heart. But no recipes have as yet been invented which would have an even approximately predictable effect on nations. Actually, experience shows that the same medicine can have the most diverse effects on two different nations. There is no political chemistry capable of equipping us with formulas and compounds of universal efficacy.

This is not what was believed in 1919, nor are people close to understanding it to-day. Those who left the imprint of their minds on the peace of 1919 had come to the Peace Conference with quite opposite ideas. They had recipes in their pockets of whose universal beneficence they had no doubt. A large portion of the famous Fourteen Points were products of this kind of chemistry. Among the recipes of that time there was, for instance, the "principle of nationality," according to which the unification of all people of the same nationality in a single state—and exclusively people of the same nationality—was always and everywhere beneficent. There was also the principle of "self-determination," according to which every nation or fraction of a nation must itself decide to what state it should belong. There was the principle of "justice" and "equal rights" for all nation, the principle of "open diplomacy"; and, it goes without saying the principle of democracy. Not every one of these and several other principles was everywhere observed to the letter. But it was believed that each of them should have been adhered to everywhere. Instances of non-adherence to any of these principles for many years served as the basis for all sorts of accusations.

The demand for such principles is human. The human mind is always looking for general rules, especially when the problems to be solved are complicated. But aside from this, there were in 1919—and there are to-day—the abstract reformers. They are the frequently attractive, but again and again mysteriously failing species whose thinking is grounded not in the world as it is, but as it should be. In their heads they have a blueprint of what this more perfect world should look like, and the universal reforms they demand are adjusted to the blueprint. They have no doubt that their fancied higher perfection would in actual fact be a higher perfection, and that it can be achieved by their reforms.

One feature of this species is particularly characteristic. It is their unwillingness to realize that everything that exists or does not exist, in ninety out of a hundred cases exists or does not exist, for very good reasons. The fact that their ideas were not followed centuries ago does not make them more critical of the wisdom of their own thinking, but more disdainful of the wisdom of the centuries—and this attitude usually makes it most difficult to reach an understanding with them. "Talk to Wilson!" Clemenceau once exclaimed. "How can I talk to a fellow who believes himself the first man in two thousand years to know anything about peace on earth?" Be that as it may, it is an essential feature of perfectionism that it inevitably must conceive the reform of the whole world in one single plan. There cannot be many paradises, but only one. The principles for the realization of paradise must everywhere be the same. But whatever the value of a principle, the aberration begins as soon as it is regarded as universal.

Could we again, as we did in 1919, regard the principle of

he national state as a universal recipe? This principle originated
in the period following 1800. It began with the struggle for
independence of the Balkan peoples, particularly the Greeks.
An immense enthusiasm for their liberation from the Turkish
yoke then swept the civilized world. This sympathy was rational-
ized. In addition to the real reason for the struggle—that Turkish
rule was bad and tyrannical—a dozen other reasons were found.
More particularly it was found that the unification of the same
nationalities and the separation of different nationalities would
everywhere constitute a factor for peace. This view has since
been considered an axiom. It mobilized the sympathies of the
world for the cause of the Italians and the Germans who between
1840 and 1870 merged into great national states. It also mobilized
sympathies for the peoples of Austria-Hungary, who aspired to
split this Empire into small national states. Such was the origin
of this principle of 1919.

Even then strong reasons existed for taking a sceptical view
of this recipe. In the light of the nationality principle, the United
States and Brazil, for instance, were simply unfortunate accidents;
these countries should have been reunited with their mother
countries as soon as possible. Switzerland should have been as
soon as possible decomposed into her three nationalities. Those
who did not want to go so far—and who would have wanted to?
—should have been forced to admit that their principle was not
one hundred per cent valid. Nor had the allegedly pacifying
effect of this principle been proved one hundred per cent true.
It was not confirmed in the case of the Balkan states which had
been separated, nor in the cases of Germany and Italy, whose
states had been united. When these countries no longer had to
fight for their emancipation or unification they began to fight
for other reasons.

All this, however, did not prevent the authors of the 1919
settlement from considering the principle of nationality a universally valid formula. The Austrian bloc was smashed on behalf
of the Danubian nationalities. In order not to separate Germans
from other Germans, the Rhineland project was never realized.
In order not to unite Germans with foreigners, Poland was
formed with an adventurous Corridor instead of a normally
constituted territory. Nothing good came of all this, and we
should heed the warning of these examples.

In theory nothing can be said against the principle of nationality. When there are no reasons against its application, it is good. But weighty reasons against its application are not infrequent. In many regions of the world a past that can no longer be changed has created a hodge-podge of nationalities. Moreover, there are sometimes more general and more vital considerations than the private aspirations of any nation. In the case of old Austria-Hungary, the preservation at a particularly critical spot of a structure with the weight of a great power was more important than the principle of nationality; in the case of the Rhineland, it was more important to make it harder for Germany to start a new war; and in the case of Poland, to create a normal organism rather than one which from the very first day was afflicted with chronic appendicitis. Let us learn to be on our guard against universal principles! A few months ago a professor at an American university created a sensation with a map of the world as it should be reorganized according to his views. It was the map of the typical perfectionist kind, and it followed the principle of nationality to its logical conclusion. Switzerland was completely erased from it—Switzerland which is a 650-year-old country, one of the very few completely successful and exemplary states. But it consists of three nationalities—so down with it! But Germany, following the same principle, was augmented by a few new provinces. Such are the absurdities to which universal principles can lead!

Our experiences with the "right of self-determination" were no better and no more promising. Once again, in theory there is nothing to say against the principle that nations—or fractions of nations—should not be pushed back and forth "like pawns on a chessboard." But here again there are necessities of a higher and more universal nature; nor is this principle by any means a guarantee of peace. In 1861 Lincoln refused to recognize the right of self-determination for the Southern states; he did this in the name of higher and more general interests. The Civil War was caused by the demand for self-determination, and the peace was concluded and had been preserved on the basis of the denial of this right. In 1919 the principle of self-determination was invoked a dozen times in favour of the Germans. Because of this principle they were completely spared certain territorial losses; others were reduced to a minimum; still others were suspended, and the decision left to later plebiscites. Peace was not served by this. Recently we have even witnessed cases in which the

ight of self-determination became an instrument of aggression
and conquest. The Sudeten Germans, the Slovaks, the Croats—
all of them could claim self-determination in accordance with the
chemical formula. But all these cases demonstrated that there
s no principle in such cases that cannot serve any purpose and
have any kind of effect, from the most beneficent to the most
evil.

We have had similar experiences with the principles of
"justice" and "equal rights." The idea that they would inevitably
serve peace is an offspring of the idea that there must be a point
of satiation for every people and every government. This is
wide of the mark. Satisfaction may or may not produce peace.
Every "objective" satisfaction may release all the stronger
subjective tendencies toward arrogance and greed and aggressive-
ness. And never can there be achieved among nations an equality
and justice which does not contain a hundred inequalities and
injustices—and every single one of them is a sufficient motive
for a war if a war is desired.

It is not even true—although this comes relatively closer to
the truth—that democracy always necessarily favours peace.
There are many eminently strong arguments to show that democracy is by far the best system of government for developed
nations. Generally speaking, it constitutes a greater obstacle
against warlike appetites than does any other system. But it is
not always an obstacle. During the last quarter of a century the
leading democracies have been extraordinarily pacific. But this
should not make us forget that each of them also knew other
times; that each of them waged wars which were clearly wars of
aggression, and waged them with the enthusiastic approval of an
overwhelming majority of the population. And the wrappings
of democracy can conceal the most varied contents. Nothing
seems so tragic in retrospect as Wilson's iron conviction that with
the introduction of democracy in Germany nine tenths of the
peace problems would be solved.

No, there is no chemistry of international relations which
would supply us with universally valid formulas. If you pour
sulphuric acid on a piece of chalk, carbonic acid is released and
lime remains. You can be perfectly sure that this will be the case
with every piece of chalk always and everywhere and under all
circumstances. Chalk is always chalk. But one nation and another
and a third: these are not made of the same stuff. Even one

nation can at different times be a completely different stuff. There is not the slightest assurance that the same procedure will produce even approximately the same effects on these different stuffs. And this is the essential reason for the eternal failure of every kind of universal perfectionism. The aims are usually very beautiful, and the formulas may be extremely suitable in some cases; but, alarmingly enough, they are not always suitable. Sometimes they are so little suitable that they produce the worst calamities.

In chemistry, as in other exact sciences, one achievement of human intelligence serves to make a thousand other exertions of this intelligence superfluous. Once a formula has been discovered, it can be applied in a routine manner, without anyone racking his brains. There is no such thing in international affairs. Each case demands the full application of our intelligence. Every nation has its own concrete peculiarities. Each lives under concrete individual conditions. A settlement that is capable of lasting within the limits of human possibility requires that we concretely and individually define for each nation what we must fear from it and what we can expect of it. It requires that we define for each nation the means by which we can prevent what is feared and further what is expected of it.

We can agree that *there is no universal recipe for peace. Each nation and each group of nations in each circumstance presents specific problems.*

Part Four: Freedom from Fear of Germany

CHAPTER TEN

THE PREREQUISITE

THIS IS A German war. Every other nation that belonged or still belongs to the "Axis" could march only behind Germany— even Japan. She was strong enough for a war against China —with her rear made safe by the excessive pacifism of the sea powers. But for the war in which she is engaged at present, her own forces are hopelessly inadequate. Only in the shadow of the German war could she undertake her own. The great problem of future security is Germany.

On one point there seems to be almost universal agreement: to be in a position to handle this problem correctly the Allies must march into Germany. Dead and buried is the hope of 1918 that everything could be done equally well from the outside or from the rim of this country. At that time General Pershing demanded in a memorandum that the Armistice be granted only after the Allied troops had marched into Germany. All he achieved in the inner circles of the American government was "frank expressions of distress." To-day not even a memorandum has to be written on this point.

But this is a coalition war, and it is not immaterial which of the coalition armies penetrates and occupies enemy territory. There has not yet been a settlement, after a war of coalition, in which the views of the allied powers did not differ. Nothing else can be expected in the present war even in the most favourable circumstances. The settlement that is finally produced will at best be the result of conflicts among more or less differing opinions. And it is clear and inevitable that the views of those allies which have actually occupied the country will *ipso facto* be far weightier than the views of those who have remained outside. The occupying power will enter the discussion with a trump card in his hand. In fact, the handling of the occupation can irrevocably prejudice the settlement.

3*

The influence our Western democratic ideas will have on the German settlement is thus dependent upon one prerequisite. This prerequisite is that on the day of victory the English and American armies be stationed on German territory; that in no case they be there in lesser strength than the Russians; and that they be there as a result of victories on the battlefield, equipped with a military prestige that cannot be surpassed by anyone else.

Then and only then will the influence of Western ideas on the German settlement be powerful. This situation is here taken for granted. That on the day of the armistice victorious British and American tanks will be reflected in the waters of the Rhine, the Weser, the Spree, the Oder, the Vistula, and the Danube is the explicit assumption of this book.

We can agree that *Germany will be the principal chapter of the settlement. Those whose armies are not stationed in Germany will collaborate very little in the writing of that chapter.*

CHAPTER ELEVEN

THE NECESSITY OF COMPULSION

"W E A R E N O T enemies of the German people and they are not our enemies," said Wilson in 1918. "They did not originate or desire this hideous war, and we are vaguely conscious that we are fighting their cause." This idea became decisive in the treatment of the German problem after Wilhelm II's World War.

A fundamental choice had to be made. To the twenty-seven states which had experienced the enormous military strength and energy of the German Reich for four and a quarter years the German problem was simple. It consisted in eliminating as radically as was humanly possible the danger of any repetition of that experience. This could be attempted in two different ways. One was the way of pessimism and the other the way of optimism. One could suppose either that the responsibility for the war that had just ended rested only on the German government, or that the German people also bore a share of this responsibility. Accordingly, the treatment of the Germans would be based either on their supposedly good or their supposedly bad instincts. In the latter case, the whole country would be put under per-

manent coercion; in the former case it would be left to live its
own life. A Germany under a certain amount of foreign guardianship, or a Germany completely sovereign: such was the fundamental alternative. The idea expressed by Wilson passed for the
progressive one. The people, the common man, is always good
—the people, the common man can never be evil: this was the
axiom of the reformists of 1919. Thus the decision was in favour
of the optimistic alternative. The treaty did not in any respect
and to any extent establish a guardianship over Germany. It
provided for the occupation of the Rhineland for a few years—
and this period was later shortened. But no mechanism of permanent coercion was constructed. It is worth mentioning that a
permanent organ was not envisaged even for the military control
of the Reich. The carrying out of Germany's disarmament, but
not the maintenance of this disarmament, was put under the control
of a foreign commission. There were violent disputes on this very
point. André Tardieu, the French member of the Peace Conference, once exclaimed: "Is it admitted that Germany, once
disarmed, can rearm? That is the question!" But that question
was dismissed in the firm resolution not to restrict in any respect
the Germans' full power over their own state.

To-day, too, we are confronted with the same fundamental
alternative. But no reasonable doubt is possible as to the nature
of the future decision. This time it will fall in the direction of
permanent coercion, inevitably.

It is true that this time, too, the opposite course is being
advocated. While the largely predominant tendency to-day is
to regard the Germans, in contrast to 1919, as a completely
hopeless case, as a people of a totally and unchangeably black
character, a small number of unflinching progressives stick to
the axiom of 1919. Peoples simply must be good: therefore the
German people, too, are good; therefore they must be liberated
from their tyrants and then unconditionally left to work out
their own democracy. This time like last time, the progressives
say that the German people "did not originate and desire this
hideous war"—and what is confusing is that this time also, just
like last time, their contention is to a certain extent true. It is
certain—and it was certain in 1919—that the German people
cannot be completely identified with their rulers. But have
psychological speculations of this kind any bearing on the
practical course of events?

The psychology of peoples is vague and equivocal. Almost every statement on this subject is a mixture of truth and untruth, and it is difficult to determine the quantity of each. And this is particularly so in the case of the Germans. I know the German people, and I maintain that no theory about that many-coloured amœba the German character can be so correct and reliable that a policy should be based on it. Whoever accepts a thesis on the psychology of the German people accepts guesswork. Twenty-five years ago the optimistic guesswork was accepted and made the basis of a policy—and the result was utter failure. The popular inference from this is to-day to accept the pessimistic guesswork. I do not think that by falling into this other extreme we shall come closer to wisdom. I think that real practical wisdom will in the end consist in not indulging in such hypotheses at all, either optimistic or pessimistic. This second time, the guesswork of national psychology should be eliminated from the business of the settlement with Germany. We are confronted with an only too familiar and clearly defined problem: the war which the extremely strong German Reich has now for the second time imposed upon the world. And within this German Reich we have a second, subjective problem: the uncertain, obscure mentality of the German people. The conclusion seems inescapable that we must direct our eyes to the objective problem, which we know only too well, and not to the subjective one, which no one really knows. Let us see to it that the German Reich remains under permanent compulsion to keep the peace, whatever the mentality of the German people.

It must be noted that if we go into psychological speculations, the evidence of the past is incomparably stronger against the German people than for them. Nothing in their past justifies the prognosis that in matters of war and peace they can be fully trusted in the future. Our experiences with the beginnings of the last two wars—not their ends; that does not count!—were bad. It is a fact that in 1914 there was no opposition to speak of against the war in Germany, although at that time such an opposition was possible. To be sure, the people "did not originate or desire" the war, but when war came they accepted it, from the Right to the Left. In 1939 their acceptance was less general. Many Germans were horrified and full of despair over the war. Only in the case of Sodom and Gomorrah did it happen that not even five righteous men could be discovered. But the thesis that the opponents of wars were in the majority and thus would have prevented it had it not been for the dictatorship is not only not demonstrable but also improbable. In 1933 the forty-four per cent who in the last democratic elections voted for Hitler knew well enough that they were voting for a future war; and to them must be added those members of the other ten German parties who on the question of war hardly differed from them. If conjectures must be made, it is far more justifiable to suppose that in all the years until 1939 there was always a large majority in Germany which was not hostile to the idea of a new war.

It is argued that in both cases the German people were misled by their warlike and militaristic rulers. This is true enough. But it is equally true that up until to-day the German people have displayed a liking for such leadership rather than an aversion to it. The overwhelming majority of them were always of fairly the same mind as the Kaiser's government and never took advantage of their legal and constitutional opportunities to create difficulties for this government. When defeat came, the people repudiated the government because Wilson had demanded this repudiation as a prerequisite for a cheaper peace. But when under the compulsion of circumstances a pacifist-civilian regime— which was never quite genuine—was set up, it soon became evident that the German people were not particularly pleased or impressed with it. As early as 1920, after less than a year and a half, the three leading parties representing it had lost their majority. The Republic lived on by dint of expedients, but the German people pressed ever more urgently for a different type of leadership. In the end they made their choice among the various competitors and picked out the most aggressive. The German people called for Hitler.

Yes, it is hard to express this fact differently: the German people called for Hitler. For although he was called to power by old Marshal Hindenburg and although some cabals were involved, his real summons emanated from the German people. They gave Hitler's party first 18 per cent, then 37, and finally 44 per cent of their votes—and these are figures which must not be interpreted in the light of the two-party system. Wherever there are a dozen parties, none of them ever achieves an absolute majority. The leadership falls to the party which is stronger than the others, and in 1933 the Nazi Party had become twice as strong as the next strongest, the Socialist. In fact, it was by far

the strongest party that had ever before existed in Germany;
and if ever the will of the German people had called a party to
leadership, the Nazis were indisputably that party. Perhaps not
everyone who voted for them knew exactly what forces he had
called to leadership, but every one of them knew that this leadership would be aggressive and militaristic.

And one must add that the widely-held notion that only
certain classes of the German people fell for Hitler while others
—the good ones, the foundation stones of the future—remained
immune to his poison is mistaken. The rise of Hitlerism gave rise
to a confused mass of false accusations, false apologies, and false
interpretations, which flooded the world. But the truth is that
the Nazis and Nazi voters were always demonstrably recruited
from all the classes of the population. They were peasants,
members of the lower, middle, and upper middle classes, professionals, white-collar workers—and they were workers, too.
According to electoral statistics, Hitler even won almost 40 per
cent of the votes of the organized Socialist workers, the Social
Democratic Party, between 1928 and 1933. There is no tenable
ground for the assertion that the class stratification of the Nazi
voters was essentially different from that of the entire nation.
Not only was the mass that wanted Hitler by far the largest
political mass ever formed in Germany; it was also a mass which
was a fair cross-section of the German people. And if we add to this
mass the parties and individuals which did not desire Hitler,
but nevertheless favoured a militaristic and aggressive leadership, we obtain a rather discouraging picture of a people which
until now has always been attracted by the same type of leaders.
They have followed such leaders when they were present, and
yearned for them when they were absent.

I know that there are explanations which put all this in a less
repulsive light—and, as I have said, even the optimistic arguments contain a certain percentage of truth. But it is clear that
if one ventures into the vague spheres of national psychology at
all, prima facie evidence speaks against the advocates of optimism
rather than for them. It is extremely difficult to interpret the
facts of the past in a way which would make us believe that the
German people have a fervent liking for peace. And what about
the future? Oh, I do not say that a favourable transformation
of the German soul is impossible—far from it! But I say that no
one can guarantee that it will take place. Very possibly the

experience of this war will leave traces on the German national psyche. It is the first time in a hundred and thirty years that the avalanche of destruction has penetrated German territory. For the first time the Germans have been confronted with devastated homes and smashed cities. Perhaps all their ideas and instincts in these matters will be altered. But what can be built on a "perhaps"?

The peacemakers of 1919 did not think they were building on a "perhaps." They felt sure. The prevalent current of opinion took it for granted that the German people, once liberated from the Kaiser and the monarchy, would enter upon the path of peace. If this had not been regarded as self-evident, the peace would probably have been written differently even then. This time it is completely clear that a peace based on confidence in the Germans' own instincts would be a speculation on a chance which may not be entirely impossible but is exceedingly vague. It is inconceivable that for the sake of such a chance the terrible risks involved in it should be accepted. For these risks are not confined to a third world war—which would indeed be bad enough—but would involve something else, too. The peaceful nations are not machines which can be turned into masses of heroes by pressing a button. They cannot be expected to defy the same inferno an indefinite number of times always in the same mood. Should they be forced twenty years hence again to wage the war for the winning of which they are now sacrificing themselves, there is a danger that they will say: If this was so futile the last time, why should we try it again? Why fight, suffer, be victorious, if it serves no purpose? I think that both the "appeasement" period before 1939 and the period marked by the "phony war," Blitzkrieg, and capitulation of 1940 can largely be explained by the fact that the peaceful nations were discouraged by a feeling that all this was useless. I know this for certain with regard to France, where I lived for many years. In the soul of this nation, which in the war of 1914 lost more than half its men between the ages of eighteen and thirty-two— not counting the others!—and which now had to repeat the same thing against the same enemy, nothing was so demoralizing as this feeling of futility. Nations are made of people, old Adams. Let us guard against involving them in subtle experiments to the risks of which they are not equal.

A third German world war would be worse than just another

war: it might very well be a war on conditions of deeper and
more widespread demoralization than this one. If we have to
practise psychology, let us heed this lesson above all! To be sure,
coercion is not an ideal solution. Coercion is only the next best
method, not the best. Better chances may be lost once the path
of coercion is taken. The exercise of permanent coercion over a
country like Germany involves worries and discomforts. And
indisputably coercion is less productive than free will. If it were
certain that in the future the German people would remain
peaceful of its own impulse, we should have to admit that this
lovely quality would develop better if left alone and not irritated
by any guardianship. Coercion which prevents possible evil can
to a certain extent also prevent possible good. But we cannot
simultaneously enjoy the advantage of two opposite methods.
As the Germans themselves put it: you can't wash a bear without
wetting his fur. We must decide one way or another. To reduce
to zero the evil with which the German nation may threaten us
in the future is our first task. If the good qualities inherent in
them cannot attain full development because of this task of ours,
that risk must also be taken. But perhaps the effects of coercion
will not necessarily be so bad as we fear. Coercive measures
strictly confined to depriving Germany of the ability to wage
war need not, as we shall see, seriously interfere with the normal
life of the country—its civilian, social, and cultural activities.
A German people which, if the optimists are justified, is animated
by a desire for peace should not prove to be too upset by the
curbing of its war potential. And nothing else need be curbed
or should be curbed.

We can agree that *no one knows the future spirit of the German
people. It is indispensable to institute a permanent machinery of coercion
that will make Germany incapable of waging war in the future.*

CHAPTER TWELVE

TOTAL DEMILITARIZATION

EVEN A COUNTRY with the strongest military instincts and
talents can wage war only if it has troops and weapons. And a
country without troops and weapons at length loses even the

strongest military instincts and talents. Troops and weapons are obviously the crux of the German problem in its material aspect, and to a great extent in its spiritual aspect as well. If German armed power no longer exists and never revives, the world—including Germany herself—will not have to fear another German war, no matter what else happens in that country.

The core of the settlement with Germany thus seems clearly defined. It is the elimination of her armed forces on the day after victory and the permanent prevention of their reconstruction. This task is different from that which it was believed to be in 1919, and as a rule its implications are not realized. But although for the moment ideas about it are vague, the general consensus of opinion seems to move in the direction of total disarmament. The Roosevelt-Churchill Atlantic Charter declared on August 14, 1941 that "the disarmament of nations which threaten or may threaten aggression outside of their frontiers, is essential."

But the general consensus seems to have a flaw which must not pass unnoticed. On November 6th, 1942 an official Russian thesis was proclaimed which is tantamount to the opposite of that in the Atlantic Charter. In his speech to the Moscow Soviet on the occasion of the twenty-fifth anniversary of the Bolshevist Revolution, Stalin postulated a difference between the Hitler state and the German state and a parallel difference between the Hitlerite army and the German army. He declared that just as Russia did not aim to destroy the German state, but the Hitlerite state, so she did not aim to destroy Germany's military power, but only Hitler's. He implied that all those holding a different opinion on this subject were illiterates. "It is not our aim," he said, "to destroy all military force in Germany, for every literate person will understand that this is not only impossible but also inadvisable from the point of view of the future. But Hitler's army can and should be destroyed."

This is surely the strongest discrepancy among the ideas of the Allies on the post-war period that has been publicly expressed. It is a discrepancy on the most important question of all. And although this thesis was surely the subject of diplomatic conversations later, it has not been corrected up to to-day. On the contrary, a number of more recent Russian pronouncements have more or less clearly adhered to the same line. And no one familiar with diplomatic texts could fail to notice that the Declaration of Teheran in its paragraph headed: "As to the Peace . . ." did not waste a single word on German disarmament.

What gives its importance to Stalin's statement is not so much the term "impossible" as "inadvisable." Whether something is possible or impossible is a purely practical question. But whether something is advisable or inadvisable is a matter of political purpose. What political purpose can be served by the continued existence of German military power, rather than by its complete destruction?

Fourteen days before the Armistice of 1918 Lord Milner, British Secretary of War, tried to convince the obstinate Frenchmen that the preservation of a certain amount of German military power was advisable from the point of view of the future. It would render good services, he said, as "a bulwark against Bolshevism." This was the first appearance of a formula which later became current. At the same time Wilson favoured the preservation of a considerable German military power from another point of view, also of the future. This power is necessary, he cabled to Colonel House, "because it is certain that too much security on the part of the Allies will make a genuine peace settlement exceedingly difficult, if not impossible." Both these points of view "of the future" proved unfortunate in the real future, and the idea of preserving the defeated German military forces to any extent whatsoever in order to use them as a pawn for political purposes proved definitely unworkable. The German army did not remain a passive thing that could be used for foreign purposes. Whatever Stalin had in mind in his version of the "point of view of the future," we cannot fail to be disturbed by the idea of letting German military power survive for any purpose whatsoever.

For what is the difference between a "Hitlerite army" and a "German army"? In 1914 there was no Hitlerite army, but only the old Imperial German army. This did not prevent it from being enormously strong and dangerous. In 1919 it was reduced and called republican. This did not prevent it from immediately setting to work in order to become strong and dangerous again, and meanwhile it was as similar as possible to the old traditional German army. In 1933, the republican label was replaced by the National-Socialist label, and the army's return to dangerous strength was accelerated. The new label did not prevent it from re-emerging as the same old traditional German army. In fact, the German army of 1944 is the army of the Hitlerite state just as the German railways, canals, and forests of 1944 are railways, canals, and forests of the Hitlerite state; but this army has as few specifically Hitlerite features as have the railways, canals, and forests.

In brief, the German army seems to have the tendency to remain what it always has been. And this is not surprising. A people with strong and uninterrupted military traditions, a people richly fertilized with the experiences and ideas of this particular type of army, is a soil which will probably always give birth to this same type of army. Should the German military tradition be interrupted for a long time, all this might be different. But within the same generation, a German army, regardless of its size or the regime or the method of recruiting, will always tend to be a continuation of the classical German army. It will be strong or try to be strong; it will be a precision tool; it will seek to be actively employed and show its superiority and heighten its prestige; and it will be the most privileged, most venerated, and most decisive power in the state. If a few generals are thrown out, their successors will not be different. If the entire officer corps is thrown out and a new one is formed, the result will be what it has always been in all the ten thousand cases of individual promotions "from below": the new officers will embody the traditional spirit even more completely than the old ones. And should Stalin imagine that the military power he is ready to grant Germany would be Communistic—well, even this German Red Army would still be a German army. The reversal of Lord Milner's idea must not necessarily bring greater joy to the inventor of this reversal than did the original idea to its inventor. Even from a German Red Army Stalin should not expect great joys. And it is quite certain that his Allies cannot expect them.

There are no straight lines in politics. It is possible that the Moscow thesis in this matter will be abandoned. At any rate one would like to trust that the two authors of the Atlantic Charter will stick to their idea at all costs. A Pandora box would be opened—or, more accurately, would be left open—should a distinction be made between a Hitler army and a German army, and should the idea of destroying the German military forces only partially, not completely, win the day. If there has ever been a conclusive experience, it is ours in this matter!

The solution of 1919 was to permit a certain amount of

military force in Germany to remain. The army was reduced to 100,000 men, and certain types of weapons were prohibited. The theory behind all this was that it would be impossible to wage war with such a small armed force. But this was a fallacy. No standing army in the world can wage war; it is only the nucleus and framework for the much larger war army. The question was not whether the 100,000 troops Germany was allowed to keep would be able to wage war. The question was only whether it would be enough to form the framework of a war army of millions. It was enough!

This was contrary to the Allied assumption. The Kaiser's standing army had been 600,000 strong. According to conservative military ideas, such a force was indispensable as a nucleus for a German war army. But it turned out that one-sixth of this number was sufficient. Unorthodox methods of "mobilization" had to be applied, and certain preparations which are made openly in normally organized armies had to be made in secret. The time normally required for the mobilization stage had to be extended from a few weeks to two or three years. But these few changes sufficed, and the smaller army (which incidentally was always larger than the 100,000 troops permitted by the treaty) performed the service that is usually performed by a standing army in the transition from a peace footing to a war footing. This smaller army supplied what is the nucleus of every army: a large professional body of officers trained in all the aspects of the trade. Man for man, it represented one non-commissioned officer corps. It studied and tested the armament problems and prepared the prototype weapons and their mass fabrication. And it kept alive and nourished the traditional militaristic spirit. The Germans themselves did not make a secret of the value they attached to this. Every company of the reduced army was, for instance, designated as the *Traditionskompagnie* of a regiment of the old army. Each company was, and felt itself, the chrysalis of a regiment, and spiritually the reduced army was at any time twelve times larger than it was in reality.

There can be no doubt that if Germany had not been permitted a 100,000-man army but only a 0-man army, we should have had no war to-day. It is extremely difficult after a long period of military vacuum to build even an army of 100,000 men starting from an army of 0 men. But it is simple to expand a 100,000-man army into a 5,000,000- or 10,000,000-man army.

A modern industrial country needs an almost incredibly short time for that. In the beginning of 1940 the standing army of the U. S. A. was only 180,000 strong. But this number was enough to be the nucleus of a war army which three years later would be expanded to millions.

The lesson of these experiences speaks to us in a loud voice. It teaches us wherein the nature of this disarmament must differ from the last one. It shows us that the crux of the matter is to conceive it really as disarmament and not as limitation of armaments. The programme must be to permit nothing, positively nothing, to survive which can materially or spiritually become the nucleus of a new military renaissance. No army, no navy, no air fleet of any size whatsoever—not one company of soldiers, not one destroyer, and not one plane. Not even a civilian German plane and not even a civilian German pilot—for the difference between military and civilian in this field is much too tenuous, and all air transportation needed by Germany can be carried on by foreign lines. No general staff, of course, no Ministry of War, no War Academy, no military attachés, and no *Wehrwissenschaft*. No manufacturing in Germany of war tools, weapons, and munitions of any kind whatsoever for any purpose whatsoever, not even of hunting rifles, revolvers, or industrial explosives. What Germany may need of these goods can be imported, and it would be better to give them to her free than to permit her to manufacture them. No barracked, militarily trained, and militarily equipped police. No veterans' legions, militias, rifle clubs, or marching or exercising private formations. No employment of German nationals as military instructors, air pilots, armaments engineers, and so on, in any country. And all this not just for a few years, but for a minimum of fifty to sixty!

In fact, the long, the very long duration of demilitarization is no less important than its completeness. For only a very long demilitarization can actually reduce to the vanishing-point the large store of technical military experiences accumulated in Germany and really break the thread of the spiritual military traditions. By A. D. 2000 the last Germans who have ever led or trained troops, or handled or manufactured weapons will have died. Even their sons who have indirectly experienced all this and have imbibed the war and army spirit through education and environment will be gray. It will be a generation of grandsons—a new generation which knew not Joseph—which has no longer learned anything of soldiering or been surrounded by armies and militaristic traditions. At that time, fifty or sixty years hence, a condition will perhaps be achieved in which Germany can be left to herself without incurring the present extraordinary risks. The grandsons of the present victors will then have to decide this question.

At any rate, no method other than complete and decade-long demilitarization can give those living to-day the certainty of having peace with Germany for the rest of their lives; and no other method offers nearly so good a prospect of normalizing the German problem for those who will live to-morrow. If it is asked whether such a complete demilitarization is a practical, technical possibility, the answer is simple. Obviously no demilitarization is easy to control. But obviously a complete demilitarization is incomparably easier to control than a partial one. Every literate person will understand that practically it is much essier to ensure that Germany has no cannon than to ensure that she does not have more than the permitted 1000 cannon. In the first case every cannon seen anywhere is clear evidence. In the second case one must first find out whether it does not belong to the permitted 1000. If it is possible to eliminate a part of German military force, it is all the more possible to eliminate all German military force.

We can agree that *what must be ensured by coercion is Germany's total demilitarization for fifty to sixty years. A partial and short-term demilitarization would be futile.*

CHAPTER THIRTEEN

THE ALLIED GARRISON

IT HAPPENS THAT we cannot undertake this project of demilitarization without simultaneously undertaking a complementary project. Only the first project interests us, but it is impossible without its necessary complement.

The complete demilitarization of Germany is impossible without garrisoning the country with foreign troops. This is not desirable for its own sake. Quite the contrary. But things have a logic of their own. If Germany has to be maintained in a state of demilitarization, the victors, whether they like it or not, must station their own military forces in the country. And if demilitarization is to last from fifty to sixty years, the foreign troops, whether one likes it or not, must remain in Germany for fifty to sixty years. There is no way of escaping this conclusion.

It is obvious that a country which cannot protect itself must be protected by someone else. This is necessary not only in its own but also in the general interest. Without doubt, Germany with all she represents will remain an extraordinarily tempting object even after her defeat. A nation which one day took possession of this unprotected country would thereby win a gigantic increase of power. Control over Germany's industry plus raw materials plus labour power plus territory would by one stroke make a great power of any middle-sized power, and the dominant power in Europe, perhaps in the world, of any great power. It is vital that unarmed Germany be prevented by all means from falling into the pocket of any state whatsoever in any form whatsoever. For this reason, lacking her own military power, she must be protected by foreign troops. And there must be an adequate number of these, and they must be stationed in Germany during the entire period of her demilitarization.

But there is another equally inescapable reason for stationing the troops of the victorious nations in Germany: without them the disarmament can neither be carried out nor maintained. A " control commission " of a few dozen people who now and then make a flying inspection visit here or there is useless. What is needed is an organization which is spread like a dense network over the entire country and whose component parts are permanently stationed at a few thousand nodal points. Nor is it enough to have a commission which has no means of power at its disposal, so that whenever it wants to do something, it must address itself to the German government. What is needed is an organ with its own executive power, which can give direct orders and whose agents can penetrate everywhere, discover secrets, stop sabotage, pursue, arrest, and punish.

If anything has ever been proved it is this. The Interallied Military Control Commission set up in 1919 to carry out the disarmament of Germany was a thing which was supposed to have eyes and ears, but no arms or fists. It comprised 337 members, who were distributed in a Berlin office and a few branch offices in other cities. There they sat without any executive instrument of their own. They had no means of physically compelling any German even to give them information, let alone of having something done that they wished to be done. The principle was: everything via the German government, which alone represented power in Germany. When the Commission wanted to investigate something, a liaison officer appointed by the German government had to accompany them; he, not the Commission, was the authority to which information had to be given, documents shown, the right to personal inspection granted. When the Commission discovered a violation of the disarmament clauses, they had to hand the records and other proofs over to the German government; it, not the Commission, was the authority that was supposed to correct any abuses. The 337 officers without troops, scattered all over Germany, were a sword without a blade, a revolver without cartridges.

The French general Nollet, who was chairman of the Commission during its first four years, later told in a book the sinister story of this control without executive power. For a short time after the defeat things went more or less smoothly. At least the Germans refrained from risking any too open obstruction. It goes without saying that from the very first day there were at every corner secret and semi-secret violations of the disarmament provisions. Only part of them came to the knowledge of the Commission. But once anything did come to its knowledge and it demanded the right to make an inspection, no great resistance was made in the beginning, and when it discovered anything in an inspection in the beginning, what it opposed was rectified without too many complications—at least formally and temporarily. But the relative willingness shown by the Germans immediately after the defeat soon changed. Within a few months the Commission confronted an occult wall of unanimous and cunning resistance—resistance by the German government, the army officers, civil servants, courts, industrialists, workers, trade unions—and for lack of executive powers the Commission could not break through that wall. The resistance began by making the inspections as difficult and fruitless as possible. It ended by following up the results of these inspections as little as possible.

"The German government," writes Nollet, "made the most stubborn efforts to multiply the difficulties in the path of the Commission. To obstruct our activities it used every possible

means. . . . It found a thousand pretexts for not giving us
certain documents we demanded. . . . It gave us others only
after a considerable delay and after having for a long time
disputed the Commission's right to demand them. . . . It took
advantage of all the artificialities of procedure." It contended
that in each case only the chief of an organization—the manager
of a factory or the commanding general of an army corps—was
entitled to give information, "and certain visits from which
results were expected were prevented by the absence of the chiefs
concerned." Likewise, the German liaison officers, without
whom the Commission could not take any action, were often
absent or intractable; in some places they refused to have any
relations with the Commission for months. The Germans discovered the trick of transporting stocks of weapons and munitions
from one camp to another so that no definite picture could be
formed anywhere. Important documents possessed by the Commission were stolen from it. In one factory "six hundred new
105-cm. howitzer barrels were discovered embedded in the
cellars with the knowledge and complicity of the workers";
the next morning the German liaison officer purloined all the
records of the hearings and never returned them—and he was
never punished. Every German suspected of having "reported"
something to the Commission was put on a black list and discredited forever, if he was not tried for treason and subjected
to a Draconian sentence. And if all these tricks did not work,
the population or workers of the places visited by the Commission were allowed to make hostile demonstrations against it—
sometimes it was met with veritable bombardments of stones—
and thus the helpless foreign officers were hindered at every step.
"These incidents," says Nollet, "did not always seem to result
from the spontaneous expression of an aroused public opinion.
Their duration sometimes seemed carefully calculated in order
to give an enterprise or army organization the time to prepare
for an unexpected visit." But most visits were expected; somehow
the people concerned almost always got wind of them.

What was revealed by the inspections then had to be acted on.
The Commission, which had no means of changing anything,
addressed its demands to the German government, and "as
soon as the control visits gave results the obstruction came from
the executive branch." The German government disputed the
findings and advanced its own interpretations of its obligations.

It argued endlessly, "clearly intending to tire the Commission and the Allied governments." When the discussion did not end in a blind alley, the measures applied were as formalistic and inadequate as possible; and at the first opportunity these half-measures themselves were weakened, "and matters already settled were questioned again." In brief, the German government "never resigned itself to the idea of reducing German arma-ments." It continually invented methods of circumventing its obligations. Most of the time the Control Commission could "record the principle" of the various methods of circumven-tion, but, lacking any executive power, it could not even "determine the extent of their application," let alone enforce their abandonment.

Such were the experiences with control at that time. True, they need not have been quite so bad even then. If the Com-mission itself had no actual power, there was always the more distant power of the Allied governments, which could at least have compelled the Germans to show more respect for this control agency. But be that as it may, the proof is overwhelming that the conspiracy of an entire nation cannot be broken by the machinery of power of this conspiring nation itself. If the organ charged with carrying out and maintaining the demili-tarization is supposed to be only the watching eye and ear, while the arm and fist is the German state machine itself, the goat is made the gardener. There is no way of preventing the thousand concealments, deceptions, circumventions, and tricks which are then possible. The decision to demilitarize Germany involves the decision to back the organs of control with their own ubi-quitous many-hundred-thousand-headed machinery of power.

It is easy to outline a plan for such a regime—and it seems difficult to reconcile people's feelings to it. These feelings are ruffled by the military "occupation" of a country, for the word "occupation" is associated with ugly, Hitlerite ideas. It evokes memories of a hard-fisted regime which has all the business of the occupied foreign country in its grip—a regime which exposes the population to every kind of arbitrary measure and burdens the occupying nations with every kind of responsibility. To expose a foreign nation to several decades of such terrorist rule and burden one's own nation with such responsibility for the same period of time is not attractive. But none of these ideas applies to the regime to be set up in Germany. Its mission would for all

practical purposes be confined to one single matter: demilitarization. And although names do not matter much it might be
advisable even to avoid the term "occupation." Let us speak
of a garrison in Germany, of a garrison force.

It can be roughly estimated that this garrison force would
have to be as strong as was Imperial Germany's peacetime
army—that is, strong enough to be distributed all over the
country and yet be everywhere an adequate local factor of
power. This army consisted of 600,000 men.

It would be natural to recruit these 600,000 men from three
200,000-man contingents of the three great powers which will
defeat Germany. A three-cornered undertaking has a good inner
balance; moreover, these three nations will enjoy the prestige
of victory, which is in itself a considerable factor of authority.
Only if one of the three victorious powers refused to participate
should we consider replacing its contingent by another—for
instance, a French one.

But it is important that these three contingents do not remain
separate units, each occupying a third of the territory. This
would breed differences and political adventures. The garrison
force should on the contrary be organized in such a way that
the three nations be mixed as closely as linguistic difficulties
permit. Each regiment, for instance, should be composed of a
British, a Russian, and an American battalion.

And it is important that the garrison force follow a code of
its own and be separated as completely as possible from its home
governments and their political oscillations and ideas. The
authorities in Washington, London, and Moscow should relin-
quish any power to give orders to the garrison force—except
the power to recall the entire contingent, or replace parts of it
by others.

It is important that the garrison force, which, for symbolic
reasons, should even have its own uniform, be under a mixed
general staff, and that every three or four years a new commander-
in-chief, chosen in turn from each of the occupying nations, be
appointed.

It is also important that the utilization of the garrison force
be determined by a mixed political authority which the victorious
governments would set up in Germany—let us call it the interallied "Peace Commissariat," whose organ the garrison would be.
And it must be added that at the very beginning this interallied

Peace Commissariat would probably be Germany's actual government; but that it would in rapid succession leave one field after another to the Germans themselves, so that in the end it would practically be nothing but the managing technical guardian of the fundamental pillar of peace: demilitarization.

Such is the plan.

Is it a plan which promises to be tenable for a long time? Yes—within the limits of what is possible on this earth and among human beings. To be sure, it will be a coalition regime, and all coalition undertakings, in peace as in war, contain germs of difficulties. One of Marshal Foch's complicated aphorisms was: "Since I have learned what a coalition war means, my admiration for Napoleon has been growing weaker from day to day." But once the principle of demilitarization is accepted, putting it into practice will fortunately be a purely technical affair and no longer a political one. At any rate, the three allies will find it much easier to agree in an institution which has one single task in one country, Germany, than in the field of general politics; and a hundred times easier than in a "world authority," before whom any question whatsoever can be brought concerning any country whatsoever. This arrangement in Germany can be durable even if the world council is not. It will answer the requirement that the institutions of the settlement should not be tied up with the fate of the world-council experiment. Moreover, even in the worst case practically the only danger it involves is that one of the three powers will withdraw. Then two powers would still remain, and they would be fully capable of continuing this regime. And, as has been mentioned above, it will always be possible to find a substitute for the power which withdrew. There is no coalition regime about which we can be as sure as about this one that it will be able to function for fifty or sixty years—and even longer than that should our grandsons find it necessary.

As the durability of such an institution seems ensured, as its organization seems simple and its need overwhelming, what could stand in its way? It is easy to foresee that what will appear as a deterring factor in this idea will be only the number of years it must endure. The occupation of Germany for "some time" and even for "some years" is to-day quite widely considered inevitable. Everyone is prepared for that—there is a consensus of opinion on this question. The terror begins when instead of a "few years" one mentions sixty. Then comes the reaction of double pity—pity for the Germans and pity for oneself. So long? For two generations? Impossible! People who feel this way would like to keep Germany disarmed for a thousand years, if possible; but they are willing to invest troops for this purpose only for a period of three or five years. Unfortunately their objective cannot be bought so cheaply. And fortunately there is no reason for pity in either direction.

No pity for the Germans is justified—not for those of to-day, who surely have no priority on pity, and not for those of to-morrow and the day after. Rigorous measures preventing them from being once again incited into a militaristic St. Vitus's dance after a short interval will in truth be just as great a piece of luck for them as for everyone else. To him who protects them from being again compelled to burn in avalanches of fire, to drown in seas of blood and to smother to death under mountains of ruins they themselves should erect monuments, regardless of the means by which this protection is achieved. But I say that the stationing of foreign troops in Germany is not only the safest of all the conceivable means to our end, but also the gentlest for the Germans. For the very reason that the protection afforded by it is total, it makes, as we shall see, many other restrictions and fetters as good as superfluous. Because this means is intensive, a multiplicity of extensive means becomes unnecessary.

Nor should those nations be pitied which will have to station 200,000 of their men and boys in Germany for fifty or sixty years. After this war, despite all dreams to the contrary, both the United States and the British Empire will in any case be forced to support much larger standing armies than before the war. Neither for the young man nor for his family will it be tragic if he spends a few months of his service period in Pomerania or Baden instead of Connecticut or Wales. It is no more dishonourable for him to belong to the great police force of world peace than for any-one to belong to the little police force of New York or London. And there will certainly be many volunteers eager to serve. Nor does the support of such a force represent a national burden of any importance. After all, these states have always had soldiers stationed at many points of the globe—it will not be a sensational novelty to have them stationed in Germany also. The idea seems strange as long as it is new and considered temporary. But it will become natural as soon as we grow accustomed to it as to a regular condition. And there is no escape from it. Nothing in this world is given us free. We must pay the price for what we wish to have. In this case an enormous price would not be too high. Luck wills it that an almost inconceivably low price suffices. To garrison 200,000 men overseas instead of in one's own country: how much less of a premium could we hope to pay for an insurance against the most terrible of all risks?

We can agree that *the stationing of an Allied garrison in Germany is essential to demilitarization. This garrison must remain there throughout the decades during which her demilitarization will have to be secured.*

CHAPTER FOURTEEN

INEFFECTUAL SUBSTITUTES AND USELESS ADDITIONS

THE CHIEF PURPOSE of the future settlement with Germany is to make another German war impossible. Other matters, too, must of course be settled, such as reparations, restitution of stolen property, and punishment of the war criminals. But these are tasks of liquidation, concerned with the past. Although they are not unimportant in themselves, they pale in comparison with the cardinal problems of guaranteeing the future. And there can be no doubt that for this purpose the demilitarization of Germany, combined with the garrisoning of the country by the Allies, constitutes the most thoroughgoing of all conceivable means. Thus the need for more artificial procedures is avoided. To use weaker and more dubious means in place of the most thoroughgoing ones would be suicidal. To complement the most thoroughgoing means by weaker and more dubious ones will be superfluous.

Some people think that we should redivide into several small states the Empire which Bismarck unified seventy years ago. To be sure, this would not be hard for the victor. It would not even be hard at first to obtain the agreement of the vanquished foe to this partition. Hans and Franz will listen sympathetically if their province is promised somewhat gentler treatment as a reward for seceding from the Reich. They would vote for it in a plebiscite. But the operation contains no promise of increased security. If Allied troops are stationed throughout the Reich, it is unimportant whether its territory is split up or not. If no Allied troops are stationed there, the partitioned Reich will, in all human probability, unify itself again within a very short time.

Let us not deceive ourselves or permit others to deceive us: the Germans feel that they all belong together. They have left the mentality of the pre-Bismarck era far behind them. In so far as it depends on them, they will live together in one state, for that is what they want. There are still many differences and much friction between the Catholic and Protestant sections; between Prussia and the south; between the west, which was civilized by the Romans, and the east, which was conquered by the Teutonic Knights. But despite all these internal antagonisms and prejudices, in the last one hundred and thirty years the German people have consistently and uninterruptedly moved in the direction of greater unity and uniformity. This is a fact. For all their particularism, the various regions have grown increasingly similar to one another in a political sense. To-day they are almost as similar as Scotland is to England, or the states south of the Mason-Dixon line are to those north of it.

Ignorance, which is the predominant factor in international affairs, has usually divided Germany into a dangerous component: Prussia, and a relatively harmless remainder. It has chosen to hope that the Germans themselves would inevitably become fed up in time with those impossible Prussians. I do not think that this theory has ever been true. Certainly it does not fit the facts as they are to-day.

Prussia has always been an exceptionally authoritarian, exceptionally organized, and exceptionally militarized state. When Prussia coveted something, she was exceptionally dangerous. But, at the same time, her mentality was of the dry, sober, narrow sort. She coveted with measure and purpose. When she had an opportunity, she now and then seized a province—as other countries have done, too. But romantic and fantastic ideas like "world domination," "master race," "Pan-Germanism," and so on, are completely alien to Prussia's characteristic narrow-mindedness and aridity. These reckless ambitions—the real dynamite, the real fuel which has fed the German evil—were, all of them, invented by non-Prussians, and some of them—strange irony—by non-Germans.

This ideology came into being shortly after 1800 with the philosopher and agitator Fichte, a Saxon; with the poet Ernst Moritz Arndt, a Swede; to a certain extent with the philosopher Hegel, of Württemberg. The great influences as the century progressed were those of the first "geopolitician," Friedrich Ratzel of Baden; the economist Friedrich List of Württemberg; the historian Heinrich von Treitschke, a Saxon. Then came the Teutonic race-fantasies of Gobineau, a Frenchman, and Houston Stewart Chamberlain, an Englishman; then those of the real organizer and apostle of the Pan-German League, Heinrich Class, a Hessian; and that great pernicious genius Richard Wagner, a Saxon and most probably a half-Jew. And there was also Friedrich Nietzsche, a Saxon and half-Pole who was most often grotesquely misunderstood, but whose influence was none the less pestilential. These personalities constitute the Valhalla of the Pan-German obsession. Prussians are not represented in it—and least of all Prussians of the ruling Junker caste. On the contrary, in old, somewhat limited Prussia these hallucinations were regarded not only as insane, but actually as subversive and revolutionary. Their apostles were often dismissed from office, persecuted, and thrown into jail. Bismarck had an attitude of cold aversion toward these extravagant fantasies.

Only in the era of Wilhelm II, and partly through the personal fault of that theatrical muddlehead, did a development take place that was later to lead to tragic results: Prussian efficiency was married to non-Prussian ecstasy. While the non-Prussians assimilated Prussia's technique, the Prussians assimilated the bubbling, effervescent romanticism that had originated among the more imaginative peoples of the Reich. Only then was that union between force and exaltation consummated which later gave birth to one fatality after another. It is impossible to determine which of the two ingredients of this marriage was more fatal, the Prussian sword or the non-Prussian extravagance. At any rate, both were necessary to achieve the nefarious results with which we are all familiar.

Nazism once more illustrates this truth. Significantly, it is an entirely South German product. It grew up in Bavaria, and there is not one Prussian among the clique of its founders. Nevertheless, its hallucinations were accepted in once sober Prussia just as completely as in their native region, and the movement learned all the tricks and stratagems of Prussian technique to perfection. By no stretch of the imagination can the Hitler regime and Hitler's war be considered "Prussian" phenomena. By no stretch of the imagination can we hope that the collapse of Nazism will unleash anti-Prussian resentment among the other Germans and lead them to break with Prussia. What our experience of Nazism teaches us is rather the opposite: that Germany has become a more homogeneous entity in the last ten years than ever before. It has shown that the irrational and rational amalga-

4

mation of the German tribes and states has advanced farther
than ever before. And should Germany be split up, there is every
reason to believe that as soon as the split-up parts are left to
themselves, they will again unite.

To be sure, after the war the Reich will be smaller than in
1919. Certain territories now belonging to Germany which are
claimed and needed by other states will not this time be denied
them. Unlike the days of Wilson and Lloyd George, at the end
of this war the peace conference will not witness Homeric battles
to prevent France from annexing the Saar, should she claim
this region, as she did at the Versailles Conference. Above all,
Poland will not be compelled to accept the bizarre "Corridor."
East Prussia, which alone can give her a unified territory and a
normal seacoast, will not this time be denied her. But there is
a great difference between cutting off certain Reich territories
in favour of a definite new owner, and the dismemberment of
the Reich into independent states just for the sake of dismemberment. The contribution of such a process of dismemberment to
securing the peace would be either inadequate or superfluous.
It is inadequate if it is the only method. It is superfluous as a
complement to the much stronger security guaranteed by the
presence of an Allied garrison. In matters which have nothing
to do with war and peace the dismemberment of Germany
would create all the drawbacks inherent in the partition of any
state. In matters directly relating to war and peace it would not
give us any new advantages.

The partition of the Reich is the most important of the
ineffectual substitutes or useless additions which are now being
put forward as guarantees of the future peace, but it is not the
only one. A measure which has recently been highly praised is
the organization of a kind of social or physical massacre in
Germany. Note well: not a massacre of Nazis and Nazi helpers
exclusively, but of entire classes and professional groups.

The theory underlying this proposal is that the originators
of all the German wars have always been and will always be
certain definite classes, and that in consequence the "liquidation" of these classes is an indispensable and reliable method
for the prevention of a future war. Which classes? The big industrialists and bankers are often named; the big landowners;
the army and navy officers; the higher officials, judges, and
university professors. What kind of liquidation? The complete

expropriation of these classes, their summary dismissal from all the posts they occupy, and their "physical extermination." If these things are not done, we are told, there will never be peace. If they are done, peace will be assured.

This recipe contains many fallacies. First it is based on the assumption that what would remain after this liquidation—that is, the German people, the German "common man"—unquestionably loves peace and hates war. We have discussed this subject before, and there is little to add. This whole argument is only a variation on the old tune about the fundamental difference between the good common people and their evil rulers. Here the bad rulers are not defined as the Kaiser and the monarchy or as Hitler and the Nazis; the definition is somewhat broader. But the gist of the matter is still that, after peeling off the diseased bark of the German tree, a magnificent trunk will emerge. We have agreed that it would be criminal once again to run the risks of this oft-proposed experiment. Nothing in our experience justifies the hypothesis that the other German classes would be very different from the liquidated ones as far as war and peace are concerend. "No matter what happens in Germany," Heinrich warned the French a hundred years ago in one of the most eloquent prophecies of world literature, "whether the Crown Prince of Prussia comes to power or one Dr. Wirth, keep your powder dry and remain quietly at your posts, rifle in hand."

Furthermore, this proposal assumes that within the classes to be liquidated all the individuals are the same. All the members of these classes without distinction are to be considered responsible for the past and regarded as dangerous for the future. This notion is even less true than the first assumption. Not only were all the other classes just as much responsible for Hitler, as "the bankers and industrialists," but "the bankers and industrialists" were just as divided as all the other classes. Among them there were the most varied types of people. Several fools and madmen belonging to these classes were for Hitler; several were indifferent; several were against him. For every one who supported Nazism another can be named who did the opposite. If Herr Fritz Thyssen was for many years popularized all over the world as one of the first Nazis—incidentally he was regarded in his own class as a degenerate fool and had no influence among them— the greatest of all German firms, the IG-Farbenindustrie, was anti-Nazi up to the last moment.

That there are people who have a passion for the liquidation of definite classes and groups is well known. And it is well known that everyone to-day links his pet notions on any subject to the discussion of war and peace. Whatever people hate to-day they denounce as dangerous for victory and for peace. Whatever anyone desires he presents as essential for victory and peace. But we must not let ourselves be talked into doing all sorts of extraneous things under the pretext that they will further peace.

The whole world agrees on the necessity of punishing, eliminating, and even liquidating those who are responsible for the war and Nazism and all the crimes of both. That this must be done, and as thoroughly as possible, without sparing anyone, is so much the consensus of opinion that there is nothing new to say about it. And plenty of industrialists, officials, and professors will be included. But there is every reason to avoid violating the elementary law that responsibilities must be individually proved, not assigned collectively to groups. Here is the line of demarcation not only between justice and arbitrariness, but between civilization and barbarism. All the great barbarisms of history, including that of the Nazis, have a common feature: the collective persecution of classes, groups, races, religions, or estates. Such persecutions have always been destructive of the ideas, standards, and customs of civilization. The new era would begin badly if the victors inaugurated it by sinking into Hitlerite cannibalism, into persecution and destruction of collectivities.

And for what? Once again, as far as barring the way to a new German war is concerned, no additional assets would thus be won. So long as Germany is garrisoned by Allied troops, we have nothing to fear from even those elements in the country in whose hearts the most warlike fires smoulder. To prevent them from agitating and teaching is part of demilitarization; but for the rest, what are generals without the tiniest nucleus of an army? They are ghosts! The complete liquidation of their instrument is as effective as would be the liquidation of their persons. What can even the most determined Pan-German industrialists or Junkers do in a country which for the space of two generations is absolutely prevented from any warlike activity? Whatever they may have done in the past, it is certain that they will no longer be able to unleash wars. They will go to their graves, and so will their sons also, without ever having had the slightest opportunity to do any warlike mischief.

And this alone is important. The spirit of the various German classes at the beginning of the demilitarization period is of no importance. During this period Germany will be fettered. The only thing that is important is Germany's spirit at the end of this era, when the question will arise whether Germany should be given her freedom again. And the spirit that we hope will prevail in A.D. 2000 will not be determined by the fate of definite classes in 1945. After sixty years, under completely new conditions, even the descendants of those classes which are allegedly more dangerous than the others may be pacifistic. This is what we hope for. But it is just as possible that by then even the descendants· of those classes which to-day are allegedly less dangerous than the others will be rabidly war-minded. By no class manipulations can we spare our grandsons the task of carefully examining the situation and deciding for themselves whether it is safe to give up garrisoning Germany, or whether they must continue to keep troops stationed there.

Some people recommend that Germany be deindustrialized; in particular, all machines must be destroyed which might serve for the manufacture of weapons of war. It would be difficult to distinguish the dangerous part of Germany's industrial machine from the non-dangerous part. Experience has taught us that in our time almost any factory can be used for war production: rayon factories can produce explosives; typewriter factories, machine-guns; truck factories, tanks. The suggestion that all the equipment that can be utilized for military production should be destroyed is tantamount to the suggestion that almost all of German industry should be destroyed. But while this destruction would be gigantic in extent—and in its consequences, also—the advantage thus gained would be nil. So long as the regime of demilitarization plus garrisons is in force, any measures of deindustrialization are completely superfluous. This regime would be able to prevent a single German machine from producing a single military tool. Only after the withdrawal of the garrisons could the destruction of German equipment, effected at the moment of the peace, conceivably influence our subsequent security. But after the withdrawal of the garrisons this equipment will be useless anyhow because in A.D. 2000 both the weapons and the techniques used in their manufacture will be enormously different from those in use to-day. The machines destroyed fifty years earlier so that they would not be dangerous at the end of the period of demilitarization would not have been dangerous any more even if they had not been destroyed. Moreover, at the end of this period, there will be no practical means of preventing Germany from rebuilding her industry.

In any case, the generation of to-day cannot possibly provide for all the problems of the period which will follow the fifty to sixty years of control. We have found a dozen times that we must leave this to our grandsons, and we shall run up against that truth very often. Everything else is illusion. And so all we have to concern ourselves with is what additional security would be gained if, during the era of absolute control, not only every type of war production were stopped, but the industrial equipment also were destroyed. The answer is that our security would not be increased by one iota, while in other respects the results would be very unwelcome. To destroy German industry means to deprive Germany of an indispensable means for feeding her population. And a settlement which would doom the German people to starvation and prevent them from returning to normal civilian life would be a fatal error. I shall speak of this later. There is no contradiction in approaching the settlement with Germany with two seemingly incongruent attitudes: Draconian rigour with regard to the prevention of the slightest military revival, and cool-headed leniency with regard to the rehabilitation of her civilian life.

We can agree that *artificial political, social, and economic measures promise nothing. They will neither adequately replace nor strengthen the regime of demilitarization plus a garrison.*

CHAPTER FIFTEEN

REPARATION FOR DAMAGES

AFTER THE LAST war it somehow became fashionable to condemn the demand for indemnities. The wealthier the nations were and the less they had suffered, the more they wrinkled their noses at those who wanted to be reimbursed for at least part of their sacrifices. People spoke deprecatingly of revenge and invoked the generous precepts of the New Testament. This attitude was wrong then and would be even more wrong after this war. A number of nations will be so ruined that they will absolutely have to be given reparations; it will be impossible to neglect their claims or deny their right to present them. Moreover, reparations and revenge can only be separated on the emotional plane, not objectively. The same book that reserves revenge to the Lord, grants man every right to demand compensations for damages suffered. It even grants him the right to punish those who injure him. Even if a certain element of punishment enters into the reparations problem, this will not offend any legitimate standard of morality. After all the monstrosities that have been committed, the urge to retaliate need not be concealed as if it were something to be ashamed of.

Practical considerations, however, sometimes forbid us to go as far as the moral law would permit. Practical considerations urge us to arrange the settlement in such a manner that in non-military respects the Germans shall not find their way back to normality barred.

One of these practical considerations deals with this side of the barricades—the victor's 'side. Man's memory is imperfect. His feelings are in a state of constant flux. To-day they are bitter, but in the course of years they will change. The wounds of the past will heal—more slowly in those who have suffered more, more rapidly in those who have suffered less. The situation of the Germans will come to be regarded less and less as a deserved penitence; it will be considered from the point of view of normal humanity. And if it is an excessively bad situation, humanitarian agitation based upon pity will begin. This is certain, for even to-day a not inconsiderable number of people are protesting in advance against any severity toward the Germans. Furthermore the regime of garrisoning will give opportunities for numerous contacts between Germans and members of the Allied nations. These contacts will create sympathy. The humanitarian agitation will swell from year to year. Bad conscience, reproaches, self-accusations, will torment the nations. Once this process has advanced far enough, Germany will again gradually become the world's pet. Once again "revisions" will begin. Once again Germany will be used as the pretext for disputes between various rival countries and between rival groups within countries. And once again, just as in the twenties, the whole structure of the peace will become brittle. This is as good as inevitable. It can be said that at length the victors themselves will be unable to endure too hard conditions in Germany.

There are no less important considerations on the side of the Germans. We cannot get around the fact that even after their defeat they will continue to exist: numerous, intelligent, and probably no less vital than before. Unlike individuals, peoples cannot be executed; nor can they be imprisoned for life. Occasionally it is suggested that all Germans should be wiped out, according to ancient recipes, or sterilized according to modern recipes; but these notions are, of course, no more than figures of speech cast to the wind. Nothing of the kind will happen. The Germans will still be here. They will be one of the great nations of the world. The decades of their demilitarization cure will one day come to an end—and what then? If we are to concern ourselves at all with this "then" for the sake of our descendants, everything will depend upon whether the cure really has been effective.

Now, this cannot be expected should the Germans have to suffer immensely during the next fifty to sixty years—suffer really, not fictitiously. The regime of Allied garrisons will enable us to prevent propaganda about invented, imagined, and shamelessly exaggerated sufferings, like that which served to arouse the Germans incessantly between 1919 and 1939, even in the periods of their greatest prosperity. In the absence of such poisonous propaganda, and if everything else goes well, they might realize that a tolerable life is possible even without world domination and martial blackmail. If so, there is a possibility that their old tendencies will gradually die out. But such a healing process is unlikely if the Germans have to live under conditions of real misery. For although, generally speaking, it is not certain in what way the human psyche is influenced by economic distress, it seems fairly certain how the German psyche will be affected in this case. The militaristic mentality may die out if it becomes clear that even in conditions of demilitarization a decent civilian life can be achieved. But if demilitarization is coupled with desperate civilian conditions, the old German spirit will be revived. As a result, while we ourselves and our sons would have peace for fifty years—which is certainly not to be sneezed at!— our grandsons would confront a Germany in an even more dangerous state of mind than she is to-day

Such practical considerations, not moral ones, dictate the

path to be taken. They compel us to find a solution of the reparations problem which will permit the Germans to recover.

What does this mean? Does it mean that no compensations at all will be possible—just as it was alleged after the last war with regard to the "reparations"? By no means. And the reparations, too, were possible. But people's heads have been filled with such nonsense on this question that even to-day the delusion persists almost undiminished that Germany suffered frightfully under the "reparations." The same tune is still being sung, and the reparations are still held responsible for all the evils that arose in Germany between the period of Versailles and that of Hitler including even the advent of Nazism. In order to arrive at some idea of the compensation that can be demanded of Germany this time, it will be necessary to dwell for a moment on the effect of the "reparations" imposed after the first World War.

The first important fact is that they had no effect at all, for the simple reason that Germany never really paid any. It does not matter whether the six instalments seemingly paid between 1925 and 1930 were big or small, crushing or barely noticeable: the naked truth is that Germany did not even pay these few instalments out of her funds. For while she paid them with her right hand, groaning loudly as she did so, the wicked world pressed approximately three times their amount into her left hand, in the form of loans and credits. As soon as these loans stopped, Germany stopped her reparations payments. In the end, Germany received payments; she did not make them.

But this is not half so intersting to us as another fact. Could Germany have paid the reparations without being crushed by them? Absolutely. Here we come to the really instructive point, which is that naturally she could have paid them only in kind. Heavy and regular international payments can in the last analysis be made only in the form of goods. Nations do not possess enough movable values of other kinds with which to make such payments. True, in appearance, payments can be made with gold or a sound international currency. But then this gold must be acquired through the sale of goods. There was no getting around this fact in 1918, and this fact shaped the course of events. For it was a fact that could arouse no pleasant feelings in England and the United States, the other two great industrial countries. These countries could not willingly accept the idea that Germany should be compelled continually to pump enormous masses of industrial goods into the world. Wherever these goods went, they threatened to cut the sales of British and American goods, to damage British and American business and throw their workers out of jobs.

The first person to be worried about this seems to have been Lloyd George. In December 1918, even before the beginning of the Peace Conference, he explained at a meeting of the British Cabinet that the reparations would inevitably result in a flood of German merchandise on the world market. "Which nation would provide the dumping ground for such goods?" he asked. The Federation of British Industries and the Chambers of Commerce do not seem to have realized this fact at the time. They were still writing expert opinions demanding very high reparations. But they learned their lesson, as did the American business men. In time a general aversion to the seamy side of reparations—that is, the deluge of German merchandise—began to manifest itself very strongly. And little by little, in both London and Washington, the idea gained ground that the most advisable thing to do was to bury the reparations, if possible.

This idea was perfectly legitimate—as legitimate as any other idea. The only unfortunate thing about it was that its motives could not be made public. There was France to be considered, and her interests were different. She was less concerned with industrial markets; she wanted reparations and was powerful enough to act on her own. The policy of gradually discarding the reparations thus could not be pursued simply because it threatened to injure British and American industrial markets. Instead, a humanitarian motivation had to be found. Hence the thesis that the reparations were ruining Germany; that they imposed indescribable privations on her people; that they were throwing the country into bankruptcy and anarchy. The same thesis was taken up for propaganda purposes by the Germans themselves, by liberals and socialists of all countries, who in part even sincerely believed it, and by the Communists, who wanted to win German support and sharpen the dissensions among the Allies. A loud chorus of lamentations over the miseries of the Germans, miseries caused by reparations, resounded through the world and led to the result we all know: the reparations were killed. The whole thing was a farce. But it engraved a second misconception about the reparations in the popular mind. To the notion that Germany really paid the reparations was added another erroneous notion: that the amount of reparations imposed was ruinous. To the question how much should be expected of Germany this time, popular opinion replies: certainly not as much as was asked last time.

But the lesson of the last experience is really quite different. This lesson is that reparations are a problem of goods. If the recipients had been ready to accept German merchandise— German merchandise delivered gratis—Germany would have been able to pay enormous damages without any serious discomfort to herself. But if the recipients were not willing to accept German merchandise, practically no compensation at all was possible. Then really nothing remained but to bury the whole idea.

There was all the difference in the world between each nation accepting its reparation quota in German goods and each of them saying to Germany: "Go to other countries, try to sell as much as you can there, and then give me the proceeds." For the first method constituted a sure procedure with fixed deliveries and fixed amounts; the second was completely uncertain. No one had any influence upon Germany's ability to sell the required amount in "other countries"; and even less upon how much of the proceeds would be available for the payments. To sell goods to foreign countries entails expenses, investments, advertisements. Nor can it be a one-sided affair: foreign countries usually do not buy unless they sell, too. Spain, for instance, does not buy German stockings in order to have the proceeds handed over to Belgium; instead she buys stockings from countries which buy her oranges. Moreover, the Allied industrial countries did not like the idea that Germany should too frantically compete with them even in "other countries."

All this, let me repeat, remained theory; it was never tested in practice, because actually Germany never paid any reparations. But in theory the problem revealed itself clearly. Without doubt Germany could have paid very much—much more than was asked of her—if payment in goods had been accepted. During the pre-Hitler era she produced about forty billion marks' worth of industrial goods a year. The highest annual instalment Germany ever paid in accordance with the "Dawes Plan"— that is, seemingly paid—was two and a half billion marks. This, and even more, could easily have been paid if the sum could have been paid in goods. Without causing any perceptible misery, some of these goods could have been dispensed with on the home market or produced solely for the purpose of paying reparations; and without causing any severe distress, the money for paying the producers of these goods could have been collected through taxation or internal loans. If any proof of this is desired Hitler himself has given it. From 1933 on he has obtained at least sixteen billion marks' worth of German industrial goods for completely non-economic purposes every year—six times more than the highest reparations instalment ever demanded. But even these much more formidable deliveries in kind, and the means of their payment, could be obtained from the German people without their sinking into the depths of misery. Since the war began, from 1939 on, the consumption of goods by Hitler's war machine has probably risen to sixty to eighty billion marks' worth a year; and even this amount which is twenty to twenty-five times that of the highest reparations instalment, could be delivered. At this point the process naturally involved a great deal of real misery and much economic waste. Nevertheless it gives us an idea of the extent of Germany's ability to produce and finance goods not intended for profitable sale. Economically there is no difference between goods given away or exploded in the air, between the production of goods intended to replace or to cause damages.

Consideration of the problem of the indemnities obtainable after this war must, therefore, begin not with an investigation of conditions in Germany, but with an investigation of the ideas of Germany's opponents. Every damaged nation must be asked: Are you willing to accept German goods delivered gratis to repay you for the damage you have suffered, or are you not? And the great industrial nations must be asked: Are you willing to permit Germany to deliver goods as reparations, or are you not? This is the crux of the problem. It is quite probable that the United States and England will accept no German goods free, or almost none, and that they will not be too eager to see Germany deliver goods free to other nations, either. Their worries about the future markets for their own industry and about the future employment of their own workers are well known. On the other hand, the Soviet Union with her ruined industry will probably need an almost boundless amount of free German goods, both manufactured goods and machines; and as a non-exporting country she will not be worried about any other aspect of this problem. Below these big three, from France down to Denmark and Luxembourg, there will be all sorts of nuances and gradations of willingness to accept German goods as reparations. The important thing is to establish a definite and clear-cut policy in this matter. The different tendencies must be discussed openly, in a business-like manner, among the nations entitled to indemnities, and reduced to a common denominator.

After the maximum amount of goods that will be accepted has been established in principle, Germany's capacity to deliver it must be appraised. An estimate must be made as to the amount of goods she can deliver year after year—for a period of thirty or perhaps forty years—without depriving her population of an opportunity to recover gradually but perceptibly. It is my opinion that under pre-war conditions Germany could have paid more than twice the two and a half billion marks which was the highest reparations instalment she ever paid. The data given above will suffice to justify this estimate. I do not think it can be seriously disputed. Under pre-war conditions Germany could have given away five to six billion marks' worth of goods without gravely suffering as a result.

However, pre-war conditions will no longer prevail after Germany's defeat. An important part of German industry will be ruined. Another part of it will be absorbed by the necessary work of reconstruction even if this is limited to the most urgent tasks. Thus German deliveries to the amount of five to six million marks will in the beginning prove impossible; even considerably smaller amounts would be possible only by dint of applying the most ruthless measures. This situation will cause a distressing dilemma in the first years after the war. In these years, the liberated countries, devastated and plundered, will need the most assistance. Not one of them will hesitate to accept German goods; on the contrary, all of them will demand the largest possible amount of them with the utmost vehemence. Yet during these same years Germany's ability to deliver will be at its lowest, and misery in Germany itself will be acute. The arrangements for the first post-war years will have to follow a particularly difficult course between the Scylla of recklessly strangling the Germans and the Charybdis of ignoring the justified demands of the occupied countries.

Later, as reconstruction progresses in both camps, the situa-

tion will become easier. It will be possible to increase the deliveries
to make them the equivalent of the five to six billion marks'
worth which could have been paid under pre-war conditions.
To-day technical reconstruction is relatively simple. After 1918,
too, the nations proved extremely resilient when it came to purely
technical reconstruction. As soon as the war was over they rebuilt
their industrial equipment with marvellous rapidity. This time
the extent of the ruin is greater; but technique has progressed,
too. In this field one is justified in expecting new miracles.

This is all we can say to-day. Only after the war, when the
necessary inventories are made, will it be possible to fill out this
framework with figures and dates, to work out schedules. Meanwhile this much is evident: the system of reparations payments
in kind can be made to function more smoothly than any other
system; for it can be organized after the perfect model the Germans
themselves have created in France. As is well known, the method
they now use to plunder France is the simplest one imaginable.
Every month the Banque de France pays the German authorities
a certain amount in French currency—eighteen billion francs
according to the latest reports. With these francs German officials,
business men, soldiers, and tourists buy whatever they wish.
With regard to individual French shopkeepers they are merely
customers. A similar procedure can be used in collecting indemnities from the Germans. The Reichsbank will pay a fixed sum
in marks to the interallied commissariat in Berlin. The commissariat will pay the various governments the quotas that have
been agreed upon. And these governments or their business men
will use this money to buy whatever they need.

A few modifications of the German system will be necessary.
Measures will have to be devised to ensure that the money is
really used for the purchase of merchandise or stock in German
enterprises, but not for improper purposes, such as financial
or currency manipulations. Such measures can be devised.
Furthermore, Germany will have to be given the means of
buying the foreign raw materials she needs in order to produce
the goods to be delivered. Every government will have to repay
a certain percentage of the money it receives in an international
currency—possibly in its own—for the purpose of financing
Germany's purchase of raw materials. The percentage will have
to be determined and modified by the interallied commissariat
in accordance with circumstances. With the help of a few pre-

cautionary measures of this kind the system will function smoothly from an economic point of view. Its smooth political functioning will be guaranteed by the presence of the Allied garrison.

Along with indemnities in the form of goods, indemnities in another economically related form may be required: in the form of labour. To a certain extent it will be possible to use battalions of German workers for the reconstruction of the devastated regions. But the fact that in this case human beings, not merchandise, will have to be delivered imposes distinct limitations on the scheme. In theory there is nothing objectionable in the idea that German workers should rebuild what German soldiers have destroyed. There is an obvious justice in this, which even the Germans themselves will probably accept —for a time. But if the "slave labour" lasts too long a time, it will cease to be accepted as a deserved punishment. Nor is it by any means certain that all the countries will be willing to avail themselves of this possibility. At a certain stage in the reparations dispute after the last war the proposal was made that a small army of German workers be sent to France to help in the reconstruction of the devastated provinces as a sort of payment on account of the reparations. As a matter of fact, this proposal was even made by the German trade unions, not by the German government. After some hesitation it was rejected. The French did not wish to have even a small army of German workers in their country. They did not wish to dismiss their own workers in order to employ Germans. French labour leaders did not want any competition from something that smacked of slave labour. All this may happen again in several countries. At any rate, indemnification in the form of German labour will not constitute an important addition to reparations in kind.

The method of paying reparations in kind will have its disadvantages. It will have to be drawn out over decades. Although these payments may eventually contribute to the realization of gigantic public works—civic improvements, roads, railroads, ports, enormous electrification and industrialization projects— they will contribute little to the most immediate, most urgent needs of the devastated countries. And in any case these countries will never recover the full extent of their damages. That is impossible. Centuries and instruments of torture would not suffice to extract from Germany the total cost of this war and the destruction the Nazis have wrought. But from 130 to 150 billion marks' worth of deliveries can be had within thirty years. This will not be negligible for the smaller states, or even for Russia.

It will even be possible to reserve part of this sum for a special purpose that cannot be neglected: the indemnification of a group which Hitler has injured in a more bestial manner than any other and which will be less relieved by his defeat than any other. I mean the European Jews—that is, those who survive, for most of them will have been exterminated before the day of victory. They were the first victims of Nazism. And they were not merely caught up in the general European disaster; in addition they were attacked individually. Without exception, every single one of them has been plundered to the last thread. And this is not all; every one of them has been torn from his social soil, root and branch. Many of them have not even a government with which they can file their indemnity claims. Nor have many among them the slightest practical prospect of building a new life, once their former native countries are restored. Of all those who have a claim on German indemnities, they are incomparably the worst sufferers and by far the most needful of assistance. They have every right to a generous quota of reparations payments.

The proposed system of reparations will give the Germans an opportunity, too. With regard to them the whole problem amounts to this: Will they, despite these unpaid exports, have enough foreign currency to import and pay for the raw materials and foodstuffs they need from abroad? The answer to this question is yes. They will have the allowance for the purchase of raw materials needed for the manufacture of the goods they will have to deliver free. They will have a free export to a number of countries—those which were neutral or members of the Axis or only nominally at war with Germany. They will probably be able to export more or less freely also to England and the United States. It is unlikely that these two great industrial countries will accept any large quantity of unpaid-for German deliveries. Finally, in the course of time, they might sell certain amounts of merchandise even in the countries to which they have to deliver goods free. This whole process will only gradually settle into a fixed pattern; it will have to struggle against enormous material and psychological obstacles; but gradually it will adjust itself. This will be accomplished through the famous economic "automatisms"; through individual connections, kinships, and sympathies which are still intact, and thanks to the zeal and skill which the Germans will certainly display. They will have a chance to earn the means with which to provide themselves, scantily at first, but gradually more and more abundantly, with the most urgent raw materials and foodstuffs. And if this much can be safely assumed, nothing else is any longer a problem. Everything else is a matter of internal financing and work—and Hitler himself has shown us how flexible these things are.

After the war a period of several terrible years will inevitably begin for Germany. But there is no reason to believe that the Germans will be unable to climb out of the abyss or that circumstances will make it impossible for them to do so. The presence of the Allied garrison will make them realize that work and sensible fulfilment of their obligations are their only chance. Thus they will be safeguarded from the pathological devices by which they ruined themselves during the period of "reparations"; from the shameless, rabid self-mutilations and self-ruinations designed to prove that reparations were impossible. They will apply their industry, energy, and intelligence to the only method which will be open to them. And it would be strange indeed if a few billion marks' worth of free exports every year prevented them from approximating the living standards of the more modest of their neighbours by the second decade of the new regime.

We can agree *that Germany must make amends for the damages she has caused, but that she must remain able to work her way up again. Only indemnities in kind can meet both these requirements.*

CHAPTER SIXTEEN

RE-EDUCATION OF GERMANY

THUS A REGIME will be established which provides for the essential repressions, but at the same time avoids useless restraints. Germany will be prevented from doing anything that might serve to fan revived militaristic ambitions. And she will be spared as much as possible from anything that might interfere with the development of new peaceful ideas. But is this all? Of course,

we expect the changed conditions of Germany's existence to
influence her mentality as well. But is it notpossible to influence,
transform, disinfect this mentality by direct action?

This is a serious question. It is natural that men should wish
to see the unique power which the victors will wield used for something more fundamental than mere supervision. The project
that is now being discussed under the name of "the re-education
of Germany" is indeed a tempting one.

I do not know how this idea arose in the mind of Vice-Presi-
dent Henry Wallace, who was the first to formulate it publicly in
the United States. Should anyone accuse me of having had
something to do with it, I would be forced to plead guilty. In
the summer of 1939, in the magazine I published in Paris, I
discussed what should be done with Germany after the war.
At that time I proposed a plan for her re-education. Some discussions followed, and it is possible that, by the circuitous route
which ideas always travel, the suggestion I made in Paris reached
Washington and inspired Mr. Wallace's proposal. And this is
somewhat embarrassing for me. For to-day I no longer recommend what seemed commendable then. A number of things
have changed. Be wary of any scheme to re-educate Germany!

In a quite general sense the Allies after their victory will have
something to say about education in Germany. They will have
something to say about it because there will be absolutely nothing
in Germany about which they will not have something to say.
This is inevitable because for a considerable time there will
probably be no German government at all, and if there is any
it will play a·very subordinate role. For instance, the Allies will
inevitably have to concern themselves with purging all institutions of Nazis and half-Nazis. The very fact that they will have
to replace the educational personnel involves a certain responsibility for the content of German education in the future.

But there is a world of difference between administrative,
technical, temporary interference and permanent control of the
whole educational system by the Allies. In the latter case the
Allied authority would have to function as the Holy See of this
system. It would have to issue the ultimate directives as to the
tendency, the "ideology," the textbooks, and the methods of
teaching; it would have to determine the philosophical, political,
and social orientation of the curricula. It would have to preside
not only over the emergency purge of the first days, but also

over an elaborate long-range programme of training teachers of all grades, and the creation of a pedagogic hierarchy from top to bottom.

If the Allies assume this task, the fact that the French can no longer serve as re-educators will become important. Unfortunately they would not be effective in this role. Their defeat—which among other things shows that they themselves need a great deal of re-education—deprives them of the necessary authority. But in the French we lose those who know and understand the Germans better than any one of the "big three." They are not only the most intellectual of all the nations concerned; they have studied Germany as no other nation has. *Germanisme,* the science of Germany, has been a discipline in their universities, just like mathematics or philology; and to a number of *germanistes* we owe the best works in existence on all the aspects of the German mentality. Furthermore, their age-old experience and constant close contact with Germany have endowed them with a relatively superior intuition about the nature of the individual German. They are less easily and less thoroughly deceived about the type, ideas, and background of the Germans with whom they have to deal; and this fact is not refuted by the Laval and de Brinon episodes, nor even by the Briand and Léon Blum episodes. The simple fact that the French will not be able to participate in any plan for the "re-education of Germany" considerably changes its prospects.

What is even more important is that instead of the French the Russians will play a role in this venture. It is impossible to imagine anything else. They will not leave this field uncontested to the English and Americans. And both the admirers and the opponents of the Russian system must reasonably agree that in no other field could a common course be less easily agreed upon than in this one. It is frankly inconceivable. We can expect that the regime of Allied garrisons will function because, and as long as, its tasks are purely technical: control of disarmament—that is the main task—permanent supervision of the reparations, and so on. But it is Utopian to suppose that the Allies could reach an agreement concerning the indoctrination of German children and adults; for at this point all generalities cease. Here the modern propagandist device of attaching the adjective "democratic" to the Russian system will not solve the problem. With what ideology should the children be indoctrinated? Shall they be told that free enterprise and private industry are a blessing or a curse? That parties and organized opposition and the right to disagree freely are essential or intolerable? That all newspapers and printing presses should belong to one owner or that the opposite of this is the ideal? That the judicial, legislative, and executive branches of the government should be separated and independent of each other or that they should be merged into one? That elections should be a process of selection among many candidates or a process of approving one single government candidate? That everyone should decide for himself whether he wants to work and where and when and at what or that this problem should be regulated by orders and prescriptions from above? We do not have to enlarge upon these antitheses to understand that it is utterly impossible to undertake a Soviet-British-American "coalition education" of the Germans. For education means the inculcation of ideologies. It should not be impossible to carry on a common practical policy in spite of all ideological differences; but it is impossible to find a common ideology in spite of ideological differences. The attempt to determine the spirit of German re-education by a Soviet-Anglo-Saxon compromise would result either in an uninspiring conglomeration of inconsistent ideas and evasions—and it would not be worth while to rear a whole generation on such meaningless stuff—or in constant differences, conflicts, and deadlocks which would paralyze educational co-operation and threaten to spread into other areas. The insoluble problem of how to reconcile Soviet ideology with that of the democracies stands in the way of realizing any project for the re-education of Germany.

It will be all the easier to give up this project since any missionary activities would of necessity be limited to schools and universities—and the spirit of a people is formed not only in schools and universities. It is also formed by the spirit prevailing in the homes of the people, and there is no way of directly influencing them. Moreover it is formed by the spirit of public life: by influences emanating from the press, the courts, the government, political movements. And at this point an alternative arises from which there is no escape. This alternative is: dictatorship or democracy. If the spirit of German public life is to be directed in an educational sense, the country must have an authoritarian administration. But if Germany is to be guided toward democratic paths, the spirit of the public life must not be directed. The alternative is inescapable, and the decision is prescribed in advance. If we want to preserve the hope that in a few decades Germany will be a normalized democracy, the formation of this democracy will have to be begun at an early date. Therefore, after a few years at most, it will be necessary to discontinue any censorship of the spiritual side of Germany's public life. All abnormal restrictions on the press, speech, and free association will have to be gradually removed. In brief, one of the most important sources of the future German mentality cannot be controlled for a long time in any case. It is not a great additional disadvantage if control in the field of school education, too, must be renounced.

Yes, democracy can be developed only by the practice of democracy. In the transitional period of the great purge the Allies will be compelled to rule Germany themselves. And it would be a mistake to open up all the sluices of democracy during this period. Since 1933 all political continuity has been broken in Germany. There are no political personalities whom the people know and who represent something for them. There are no longer any parties that express a definite tendency familiar to everyone. All knowledge of developments in the outside world is entirely lacking. Under these circumstances it would be very wrong to let loose a hurricane of political agitation over Germany, to let the new political figures and new political groups rush down upon the unsuspecting people in wild competition and through uncontrollable formulas enlist them in unforeseeable causes. Obviously the sluices must be opened only slowly and gradually in order to give the people an opportunity to get their bearings again in the new situation. They must have a closer look at the new leaders and new labels that are offered to them.

But then, step by step, the Allies will have to turn the administration of the country back to German agencies. Step by step the freedom of press and speech will have to be extended again. Step by step political parties will have to be allowed to organize, and elections to representative bodies will have to be held. This is necessary for many reasons. Among other things it will enable us to appraise the development of the German spirit. How could the Allies gauge this spirit if their authoritarian regime did not permit it to reveal itself?

Let us hope for an indirect education of this spirit, for its reformation by new conditions. These can have a considerable effect. The still voice of power is eloquent for all nations, but particularly for the Germans. Privately and collectively they have always displayed a great gift for adapting their ideologies to the regime under which they have lived. In 1919, when they thought that an obstacle of granite forever barred the way to new adventures, four-fifths of them adopted a pacifist, good-neighbour ideology. When they realized that the obstacle was not of granite, but of wax, they sloughed off their pacifist skin; they grew progressively more militaristic and bellicose. There is a strong probability that this time, too, the German spirit will adapt itself to the circumstances. The presence of a foreign garrison, and a few drastic examples that not the slightest evasion will be tolerated, will have a powerful effect on the mentality of the people. Confronted with the certainty that no other path is open to them but a peaceful one, they will not only put on the exterior trappings of a peaceful ideology, but actually adopt it. But even should our hope of this transformation prove vain, no danger will threaten us. The world can still feel secure. The garrison will be there, at the ready. Nothing can happen. And it will soon become clear in what direction the spiritually un-hampered German democracy will evolve.

We can agree that *the purging of the German spirit can be expected to take place only as a result of the new conditions of power. Organized re-education by the victors is impossible and undesirable.*

CHAPTER SEVENTEEN

THE REST OF THE AXIS

NO COMPARISON is possible between Germany and her allies of to-day and yesterday. Japan and Italy represent another order of dangers, other problems of control. Certainly, the settlement with them also must as far as possible be such that it can subsist even without the successful functioning of a world authority. If the world authority stands the test, we shall have a general guarantee; but what we are trying to find now is special guaran-tees in the event that it does not stand the test. Now, it is clear that we require from neither Italy nor even Japan the same special guarantees as from Germany.

Before this book is published, Allied public opinion will perhaps consider Italy more as a rewon ally than as a vanquished enemy. But even before the armistice with Italy it was clear that her case had to be viewed in a different light from that of Germany. Regardless of the events of September 1943, it would have been advisable to shape the future status of Italy more like that of the liberated nations than that of Germany. And this not for sentimental, but for military reasons.

Italy has a larger population than England; yet in the course of this war it has become completely clear that she is only a fifth-rate military power. This is a result of her irreparable industrial weakness. A country without iron, coal, metals, and oil is, under modern technical conditions, simply not a military power. This explains the ghostly role Italy has played in this war: the main cause was her painfully inadequate industrial war potential. The industry that Italy has is good; her technicians are talented; the weapons she produced were of fair quality— and she produced some of each kind of weapon. But quantitatively her output was just enough to decorate a show window, sufficient for a little bluffing. When the bluff was called, her equipment did not suffice for anything. Thinly spread over the divisions, it sufficed neither to win the operations that had begun nor to begin operations that could have been won. This was true in regard to planes, tanks, artillery, heavy munitions, transportation. And this is the military reality of Italy. In the future this will be even more clearly marked, for the industrial aspect of war will continue to grow more and more important.

For this reason Italy, since her *risorgimento*, has dared to wage only two insignificant wars by herself: the Ethiopian expedition of 1895 and the Tripoli expedition of 1911. And even these were undertaken only after she had obtained the formal consent of all the European powers. In every other case Italy was only, as the unfriendly phrase has it, a "jackal" marching behind belligerent great powers: in 1856 behind France, in 1866 behind Prussia, in 1915 behind the Entente, in 1939 and 1940 behind Hitler. Yes, even her Ethiopian campaign of 1936, although seemingly waged independently, was in reality undertaken by her only because she was a hanger-on of the big beasts of prey, Hitler and Hirohito; because, in fact if not in form, the big powers were already waging war among themselves. In short, history shows two things: modern Italy has never felt strong enough to attack a great power single-handed; and she has felt herself in a position to attack even a small power only when she first secured the consent of the great powers or when these great powers were fighting among themselves.

It follows that special guarantees in the case of Italy are superfluous. A regime of permanent control such as is necessary for Germany would here be only a useless expense. The only guarantee that is necessary and possible is contained in the permanent law of all Italian politics—the law which is so inherent in the physical limitations of the country that even Mussolini was subordinated to it. This law is that Italy can wage war only in the shadow of wars among the great powers. If the great powers live at peace with one another, they do not need to control Italy. If new conflicts arise among them, they cannot control her.

The armed presence of the victors in Italy will be necessary and desirable for some time. Here, too—just as in Germany— the sudden jump from a political vacuum into a full-fledged democracy might lead to disaster. Here, too, the correct procedure is to give the people some time to see their way clear. But this transitional stage need not last long. Through Churchill's mouth the Italian nation had been guaranteed "the untrammelled right to make what arrangement it chooses for the future government of their country on democratic lines, when peace and tranquillity are restored." In this sense tranquillity can be restored one or two years after the peace. Elections, the meeting of a new parliament, and the formation of a government by this parliament will then be possible. And while certain nuances of this democracy may be significant from one or another point of view, they will be quite unimportant from the point of view of war and peace.

Frankly speaking, I cannot believe that they will be important from any point of view. The dynastic problem—that of the House of Savoy, not, of course, of the impossible King— which has aroused so much discussion seems to me largely irrelevant. Whether democracy be in the form of a monarchy or a republic is in our time no longer a great issue. It has been demonstrated often and clearly that democracy can function in both forms and be ruined in both forms. Crowned George and Gustave and Wilhelmina have not been more harmful to democracy than uncrowned Poincaré and Roosevelt; and republicans like Hindenburg, Pilsudski, and Castillo have not fostered it more than kings like Boris and Victor Emmanuel. It is an illusion of the conservatives that the preservation of the House of Savoy will ensure a conservative future for Italian democracy; and it is an illusion of the radicals that the deposition of the House of Savoy will ensure a radical future for her. Whether a democracy will march or be pushed, to the right or the left, to peace or to chaos, to glory or to bankruptcy, cannot be determined by any arrangements made in the first hour of peace. *La democrazia farà da se.*

Darker, more disquieting, more mysterious is the problem of Japan. There are probably not even fifty white men of whom it can be said that they really know the Japanese soul, the Japanese mind, instincts, traditions, and reactions. We are confronted with riddles. How will Japan's mentality evolve after a defeat— the first ever suffered by this country? To what extent does this strange mentality allow of any hope for normalization? Has a regime other than the half-religious one of the Midako any prospects? Where can the victors find cadres to rule this remote country? How could collaboration between the Anglo-Saxons and the Chinese — who do not lack strangeness, either — be organized in such a regime of control? Only those who have the necessary knowledge and experience of the Orient can answer these questions.

But aside from all spiritual riddles two sober unambiguous facts may serve to give us a general orientation.

First, after the war we shall no longer have to deal with a Japan of the present dimensions. Japan will again be confined to the islands which constituted her territory before 1894, the date when after a thousand years of slumber she entered upon her era of conquests. The empire which to-day rules over some three hundred and twenty millions, which before Pearl Harbour ruled over some two hundred millions, and before the beginning of the present war with China over some one hundred and forty millions, will again be the Japan of fifty years ago, a state of seventy million Japanese and no one else, a state extending over its original islands and nothing else.

Even then the Japanese will still be a numerous people. But they will again be a people who—like the Italians—are deprived of all important military raw materials. Japan will no longer have iron, coal, metals, and oil; for all these things, and many others, are to be found only in the regions she has seized during her fifty years of expansion. Likewise Japanese industry will be cut to a fraction of its present size. And it is clear that Japan will thus cease to be a first-rate dangerous military power. She will not even approximate Germany in power. With regard to her, less stringent special guarantees should be sufficient than with regard to Germany.

Secondly—and this is another important difference between Japan and Germany—she will consist of nothing but islands; she will not have the slightest foothold beyond her shores. This means that she will no longer be able to march forth to war, but only to sail and fly to it. To wage any kind of war she will have to use sea lanes and air lanes. If she is rendered incapable of using these lanes, she will be incapable of waging war—even of waging war with a land army. For a nation that has no way to reach another nation is non-existent militarily. England without her navy and air force and without sea and air lanes would be non-existent militarily.

Thus the Japanese problem, as compared with the German, seems to be further facilitated, from a purely technical point of view. It will perhaps be possible to limit the special guarantees to naval and aerial disarmament and the establishment of a sea and air police. Fortunately, this is a much easier task than the disarmament and control of land forces. Ships on the water and planes in the air cannot be concealed. To control demilitarization on land, an army of occupation is necessary. But to control naval and aerial demilitarization a few patrol warships and planes with a few local bases are sufficient.

We can agree that *special guarantees with regard to Italy would be useless. In the case of Japan naval and aerial demilitarization should suffice.*

Part Six: The Other Side of the Barricades

CHAPTER EIGHTEEN

THE LIBERATED NATIONS

HISTORY TELLS US of wars started by every known nation. The future peace is threatened not only by the defeated: the victors and the liberated countries can break it, too. Can we find means to keep these nations too, in check?

The case of the liberated nations is simple as long as the big three—with or without a world council—remain united in their resolution to prevent war. It would be monotonous to repeat that the liberated nations, like the rest of the world, would then be effectively prevented from waging war. True, one of the liberated nations, France, will again have a respectable war potential. Nevertheless, it is now clear that neither numerically nor industrially will she be equal in rank to any of the big three, and certainly not to the big three combined. Even France will find it almost completely impossible to embark on any adventure; and the other liberated countries will find it even more so.

But once again the question is: Can means be derived to secure the peace if the unity of the big three—or the world council—is broken? Is it possible to write the settlement in such a manner that even in this case the liberated nations will be prevented from waging war? Or in such a way that the causes for war will be removed? Can we, in this case, too, have special guarantees, other than the projected general guarantees?

It can be seen at once that the most effective of all the special guarantees is clearly inapplicable in the case of the liberated nations. There can be no question of their demilitarization. That would be absurd—their armies are needed. To be sure, they will not be needed as long as the three big nations are in agreement. As long as they are, these armies will—in theory—be useless both for their own nations and for the rest of the world. But they will be important if the agreement among the big three is broken. A French army is indispensable in the very eventuality for which we seek a special guarantee, and with it, the smaller armies. Then they will be necessary not only to protect their own countries, but also for the world as a whole, as reinforcements, as replacements, as factors in a new balance of power, as foundations of a new wall of security. This is the meaning of Churchill's repeated assurances that "it is one of the main and enduring interests of Great Britain in Europe that there should be a strong France and a strong French army." It is not only an interest of Great Britain. The disarmament of possible allies is not a good insurance against war.

But it is useful to explore this absurdity one step further. Obviously none of the liberated nations will agree to disarm of its own free will. None of them will consider it fair to be placed at a disadvantage in relation to the big three. Such disarmament could be enforced and maintained only by compulsion— most probably, just as in the case of Germany, only by occupation. This is impossible if only for practical reasons. The British and American peoples will not agree permanently to occupy entire continents. But this brings us to a wider, more comprehensive subject: Beware of compulsion! Beware of treating the liberated nations like the defeated nations in any respect or to any degree. Beware of anything that looks like diminution of their sovereignty or tutelage by the great powers.

The temptation to use compulsion will be great. The liberated nations will be weak and will need help. Allied armies will be stationed on their territory. And the very desire to improve the world creates the inclination to exert pressure on all sides, to promulgate rules and precepts. It would be disastrous to yield to these temptations. There can be no worse way of inaugurating the new era than by failing to respect the right of the liberated peoples to act according to their own free will. They have no reason to concede that any of the big three possess superior wisdom and morality. On the contrary, they are all strongly convinced that the great powers are more responsible for the catastrophes that have taken place than they themselves are. As they read the record they are creditors rather than debtors. They will be all the more irritated by any attempts to push them or order them around. Instead of feelings of kinship and unity such procedures would create resentment and ill will. Yes, we may go even farther and maintain that too many sermons, too much advice *du haut en bas* will create resentment and ill will. An excess of good advice is enough to ruin any friendship.

In the future, just as in the past, the French and the Dutch and the Greeks and the Norwegians will do many things less wisely or efficiently than they could be done. Now and then it may even happen that some enlightened foreigner will really know a better way to do what must be done, for not all those who think they are enlightened are really so. Wilson was by no means justified in saying to the Italian Prime Minister: "I know the Italian people better than you do." Nevertheless, even those who could justly say such things do not usually do any good when they try to push foreign peoples along a path which is the path of wisdom, but is not their own path.

Glancing back at the tragic history of the peace of 1919 we see that a not inconsiderable cause of its failure was Wilson's tendency to assume a tone of moral superiority, a "holier than thou" attitude. This was neither convincing nor, more important, attractive and likely to produce unity. Yet he was moderate compared with an army of lesser reformers and zealots active at the same time and later. Indefatigably, for years on end, they kept hammering their allegedly higher wisdom and nobler morality into foreign peoples and governments, in lectures and newspaper articles, showing a special predilection for France and pre-Fascist Italy. They did not realize how much aversion, animosity, and hostility they aroused. Even to-day it is not sufficiently understood to what extent this policy of didacticism and moralizing contributed to the estrangement and disunion of the Allies of yesterday.

May this experience—which is nothing but a confirmation of the most elementary common sense—deter us from repeating such mistakes. Hands off those whom we want and need as friends! They must have the same freedom and independence in their own affairs as the big three have in theirs. Only so much interference, material or moral, in their internal organization, political life, traditions, and possessions should be permitted as the big three accept for themselves. True, there is no political principle for which absolute validity can be claimed. In certain special cases the internal affairs of a country can really become the concern of the whole world. If, for instance, an extremist military dictatorship is set up in a very strong country, this fact has more than purely domestic significance. It represents a tangible and serious threat of war, which not only justifies intervention from outside, but makes it imperative. Such was the case of Germany in 1933. But even in strength alone none of the liberated countries can be compared to Germany. In none of them can any political development capable of becoming a threat to world peace be foreseen even on the most distant horizon of practical possibilities. And so let no one presume to meddle in their business, either by placing them in permanent tutelage or by exerting pressure on individual decisions, or even by too much public preaching and teaching.

There are no real indications that the governments of the United States and Britain have a different opinion on this question. They have often guaranteed, to quote Churchill once more—"full freedom to the French nation as a whole to decide its future destinies under conditions of peace and tranquility." Indeed it is difficult to imagine what else they could do than sooner or later leave the French to their own democracy. And because this is so, all the noisy debates and backstage intrigues over the stopgaps of the transition period—Giraud, de Gaulle, and other "expedients"—are just as pointless as those over Badoglio and the House of Savoy. The desire behind them, both on the Right and on the Left, is to chart a definite course for French democracy in advance. This desire is futile. Although temporary measures have been necessary in the past and will be necessary again, they will not decide anything finally. In almost all the liberated countries—just as in Italy and even Germany— the Allies, who will be in control of state power, will perhaps be forced to serve as midwives at the birth of the new democracy. They may have to see to it that the first elections do not take place while people's minds are still in a state of grave confusion; that they take place under conditions of freedom, under the ægis of a provisional government formed on an equitable basis and representing all important tendencies. But once the new democracies are born, they will take their own course. And God forbid that they should be pushed, shoved, molested, or hampered from outside. The effects of this might be exactly contrary to those expected.

Other, perhaps even more dangerous, ideas are in circulation. From curiously disparate sections of public opinion comes the oft-repeated dictum that an important object of the coming settlement must be the colonies. In some form, to crown the achievement of this war, Holland, Belgium, France, and, of course, England should be compelled to give up their empires.

For some reason this is considered important for the peace of the world.

Unfortunately, the exact definition of a colony is still lacking. It is still incomprehensible why India, for instance, should be considered a colony, but not Siberia. The former was taken over by England during the seventeenth century, the latter by Russia at about the same time; and both are in Asia. The only difference seems to be that in one case the conqueror was separated from his conquest by water, in the other by mountains. No, there is still another difference: the Siberians were never given an opportunity to express any kind of opposition; the Hindus received such an opportunity. Then what is a colony? Something that is separated from its mother country by water, but not something that is separated from it by mountains? Something that has been treated in a liberal spirit, but not something that has been treated in a Draconian spirit? This question deserves to be clarified. For it might turn out that there are many more colonies in this world than we think; and the present passionate desire to free them might cool off considerably.

But aside from this, the problem is disquietingly ambiguous. For it is not enough to speak abstractly about the colonial peoples and their freedom. It is also necessary concretely to investigate each case and its possibilities.

To-day there are no longer any colonial peoples at the level of development the population of the thirteen American colonies had attained in 1776. Those who have reached this stage have long ago ceased to be colonies. What would be the results of liberation for the real living human beings who inhabit the colonies of to-day? Would the individual Dutch Indians or French Arabs be better off in any respect? In all probability the answer to this question is no. Torn from a stable and relatively wise white administration, they would become the prey of struggling and probably more savage native contestants for power. In place of the civilized legal system which—often for the first time in their history—has given them elementary standards of justice and personal inviolability, they would probably be subjected to a much more oppressive and arbitrary rule. What is at worst mild "exploitation" within the framework of powerful economic and cultural advances would probably be followed by much more unbridled exploitation at the hands of native rulers within a framework of general economic regression.

It is an incontrovertible fact that the Arabs in the French colony of Tunis, for instance, live under incomparably better and more dignified conditions than those in free Saudi Arabia.

This is true of most colonies. Almost all the existing colonial populations have not lost but benefited from colonization. And in general, during the last few decades, the various colonial administrations have been improved to such an extent that the old-fashioned ideas of the horrors of "colonial imperialism" no longer correspond to the facts. Of course, everyone is still free to stick to his principles and proclaim: *Liberté quand même!* This is a position that can be defended. But it must be understood that such a position implies accepting inferior realities for the sake of superior principles. Surely we can say without irony that in a shattered world reforms of such a dubious nature cannot be considered the most urgent.

What the "colonial problem" has to do with war and peace is least clear of all. Why should the continued existence of colonies produce wars and the elimination of colonies further peace? Did the Japanese pounce upon the East Indies because they were a colony? No, they pounced upon them because they were the East Indies. Was Hitler prevented from pouncing upon Poland by the fact that Poland was not a colony and possessed no colonies? Obviously not. Conquerors have never shown the slightest preference for colonies or independent states, for nations possessing colonies or nations not possessing them. Without prejudice they grabbed whatever they could grab. Not even the most fertile imagination can show why or how the liberation of the colonies would make the world safer for peace.

There is only one obvious connection between the colonial problem and war. At the end of the war should a serious attempt be made to "solve" the colonial problem, the outlook for peace will be poor indeed, and international unity will almost certainly be destroyed. If pressure is put upon the French, Dutch, Portuguese, Belgians, and of course the British to give up their colonies, unpredictable forces will be unleashed. For although within each of these countries there has always been a minority that supported the renunciation of the colonies, it was only a minority —and in reality the subject was academic. There are reasons to believe that even this minority would evaporate should the question be raised seriously. In all these countries a practically universal movement of resistance would arise. The peoples concerned would consider it a monstrous injustice that after suffering the depredations of the enemy for years, they should have to consent to being robbed by their friends. It is unlikely that the liberation of the colonies could be carried through in the face of this embittered resistance; at any rate any hope of future solidarity among the nations which to-day call themselves the United Nations would be buried. A smouldering emnity would remain. The new peace could not be strengthened; on the contrary, it would be poisoned from the beginning. Let us avoid any such undertakings; let us even avoid agitating too much for them.

Sane and equitably drawn frontiers are also very often regarded as an effective special guarantee against war. Sane and fair frontiers, many people believe, particularly between the smaller states, would make the peace more enduring.

In 1919 this hope was strong. Believing that it was possible at last to discover such frontiers, Wilson took with him to Paris a miniature research institute for history and ethnography. Volumes of weighty, scientific expert opinions were written about the proper frontiers between France and Germany, Italy and Yugoslavia, and dozens of other countries. What a hopeless undertaking! Between old countries like those of Europe there are always mixed zones. Every frontier imaginable can be called unjust by one party or the other or by both. But even if there were such a thing as a just frontier, it still would not constitute a brake against war. Increase of power is the purpose for which wars are waged. The injustice of the frontier only plays the role of a pretext, a means of propaganda. If this pretext were absent, another would be sought and found.

Other people think that federations or unions of small states can constitute a bulwark against wars. These people also err.

Such unions are indisputably desirable for many reasons, particularly economic ones. Whenever two nations spontaneously desire such unions, they should be encouraged. But one cannot help remarking that it is only rarely that nations really desire to unite. Those of us who are old enough can still remember that a certain union which had been realized was dissolved again —and it had seemed to be a particularly natural union between two highly civilized nations; I refer to the separation of Sweden and Norway in 1905. In such developments factors are operative which have nothing to do with rationality. No genuine movement for unification has arisen among the little nations. Almost all

5

the existing projects for unions have been worked out behind some dreamer's desk. Above all, in the Balkans and the Danubian countries, where unions would be most desirable, they have not been strongly desired in the past, nor is there any indication that they are desired to-day. This is not a promising prospect; for in this case, too, it would be inadvisable to force anything from the outside. It is ominous enough that the only project originating among the nations concerned—the Czech-Polish project—has been blocked by Russian opposition. However, this does not change the fact that to impose such projects upon the little nations would be equally unsound. The partners themselves must decide whether they want to be united. Regrettable as this may seem, the future of all the projects for federations remains problematical.

Regrettable, yes, but again not from the point of view of war and peace. The truth is that, at best, unions put an end only to wars between the members of the union. But the danger which is eliminated within the union will continue to exist at its frontiers, and may even be increased as a result of the union. The history of all states is a history of progressive unification. Cities and provinces which once were independent, and fought one another, little by little became unified, and thus the states we know to-day were formed. But wars did not cease. They took place on a higher level with each stage in national unification. They grew less frequent, but bigger and more far-reaching in their consequences. Federations do not ensure us against the possibility of war; they only change the nature of the various possibilities of war.

Let us, then, pray that the great victors in this war will not try to prescribe the path of the liberated. Certainly every rule has its limits. Freedom of speech, Justice Holmes said, does not mean that you should be entitled to stand up in a crowded theatre and cry: "Fire!" Every freedom has limits dictated by the general interest. All attempts to define these limits precisely and universally have so far failed miserably. But even if no one can define these limits exactly, they are clear enough for all practical purposes. Roughly speaking, it is a reliable rule that the liberated nations should not be enforced to accept anything which the big three would not be willing to accept themselves. The same respect should be shown for their personality that the liberators demand for their own. They must be made to feel that in the Allies they have reliable friends; and that, because the Allies understand their own selfish interests, they will give them all the help that can be given.

We can agree that *the only means of imposing peace upon the liberated nations is harmony among the big three. There is no substitute for this harmony if it is destroyed.*

CHAPTER NINETEEN

THE BIG THREE AMONG THEMSELVES

THE DEFLATED AND liberated nations can be prevented from waging wars by the big three. The big three can be prevented from waging wars only by their own will for peace. No other guarantee can be found; no preventive measure can be taken against the possibility that one of the three will become aggressive. The aggressor may ultimately be defeated; his appraisal of his chances of success may prove false; but this will be proved only through war.

From a purely mathematical point of view, six cases of war within the family of the big three are possible, three between two of them and three involving an alliance of two against one. Fortunately, reality is less threatening than mathematics; several of these possibilities can be excluded as completely improbable.

In the real world we can fortunately rely with full confidence upon peace between England and the United States. More than that, no other two nations can be more safely expected to work in close harmony. True, some traces of the old animosity between them still remain. But the trend of the times is decidedly in the opposite direction, and the new shape of things is creating a new psychology. Even in the past the political and economic realities had brought about that development which Mr. Walter Lippmann has recently drawn to the attention of the public: for generations there has been fundamental agreement in the international field between the English and American governments— independently of and even against popular ideas on the subject. In the last two decades this agreement has become strengthened on almost every detail: there is hardly an important international question with regard to which the two Anglo-Saxon countries have not taken a common line during this period. Significantly enough, they even shared the same errors and illusions, as for instance in the matter of the Japanese invasion of Manchuria in 1931. As can be proved by the record, even then the two countries were completely unanimous in their decision not to apply force against Japan in any case. And this constant harmony has been based not on agreement and treaties, but on similar interests and, above all, on similar ways of thinking and feeling.

In more recent times their common fear of isolation has brought the two countries even closer together. Both of them have awakened to the feeling that the world is too full of dangers for any country to face it alone. In seeking reliable allies, each has discovered that the other is by far the most suitable. No other two countries in the world are so clearly predestined for close association as the United States and Great Britain, because of their common language, law, literature, and way of life. No wonder that at present the discussion has gone far beyond the idea of co-operation to the idea of a formal alliance. If this alliance were formed, it would be a tremendous event in the history of mankind, whether or not a world authority is created in addition to it. But even without this alliance we may certainly expect a considerable degree of co-operation between England and the United States. The possibility of a war between them is obviously remote; for all practical purposes we may exclude it in advance.

There is something else that for all practical purposes can be assumed as certain: just as surely as England and the United States will not wage war against each other, so they will not seek an armed conflict with Russia or provoke her to start one. This is being proved by their general policies in the international arena and by the history of their relations with Soviet Russia in particular.

For forty years now Britain and America have manifested a complete lack of international "dynamism." They have not sought to expand. They have not displayed any crusading spirit. They have avoided like the plague every possibility of war, whatever its cause. They have not wanted to impose anything on other nations or to take anything away from them. They have desired intensely to be left in peace by other nations. And in order to be left in peace they have been ready to pay the

highest price. In all their acting and thinking they have represented the conservative, static, contracting type of nation rather
than the expansive type. And even to-day, amidst war and war
emotions, there is not the slightest symptom pointing to any
change in this fundamental trait. There is no kind of annexa-
tionist movement in either of these two countries. Outside the
Left—from which certainly no danger for Russia will come—
there is not even a movement for the expansion of ideologies,
nothing that could be compared even with the shortlived
enthusiasm which flared up under Wilson for "making the
world safe for democracy." These two nations are waging
war for their old international ideal: in order to create conditions in which they will be left in peace. It is practically
inconceivable that after the end of this war they will want to
be aggressive toward anyone for any reason, directly or
indirectly.

With regard to Russia, too, they have demonstrated this
desire to be left in peace and nothing else. Indeed, as far as
she is concerned, they demonstrated it on one occasion in a
particularly striking manner—one might say in a historically
sensational manner. This occasion was the "intervention"
of 1919, of which many people have a scurrilously distorted
idea.

In February 1918, when the young Soviet regime capitulated
to Wilhelm II, the internal rift in Russia gained added significance; it was no longer merely the opposition between Bolsheviks
and anti-Bolsheviks; it was also the opposition between war and
peace with Germany. The Bolshevik territories had broken away
from their alliance with the Allied powers. Behind a paper line
of demarcation they lay defenceless against exploitation by the
Germans. But the anti-Bolshevik territories, living under almost
twenty different governments of every shade from Red to White,
refused to recognize the capitulation. They remained in the
alliance and at war with Germany. Thus, from the point of
view of the war against Germany, it was necessary to maintain
connections with these territories—de Gaulle territories, so to
speak—and support them against Moscow. In June 1918, Allied
troops were landed at the three ports of Archangel, Murmansk,
and Vladivostok. At this time, when decisive battles were raging
in France, the Allies could not spare large numbers of troops.
The contingents sent to Russia comprised in all three divisions,

and this number was never increased. Few arms could be delivered to the anti-Moscow Russians. There was only a trickle of them. But within these modest limits the expedition fulfilled its purpose.

The war with Germany ended in November 1918. Operations that had been necessary in connection with this war were no longer necessary now. The question arose: What was to be done about the regiments stationed in Russia and the deliveries of arms to the anti-Bolshevik troops? Two conflicting opinions were voiced. Wilson and Lloyd George were for recalling the expedition and stopping all collaboration with the anti-Bolsheviks. Let the Russians settle their own business! Churchill and Foch wanted to strengthen the expedition and send more support to the anti-Bolsheviks. Let us change the anti-German intervention into an anti-Bolshevik one and bring the Russian struggle to a decision.

The outlook for the Soviets was bad at that time. The area over which the red flag then flew was no bigger than the Duchy of Moscow in the sixteenth century. Lenin's government in the Kremlin no longer controlled Siberia, the Urals, the Caucasus, or the Ukraine. If 100,000 men had been added to the Allied corps in Russia and the armaments supply increased somewhat, it would have been possible, according to the generally accepted view, to deal the death blow to Bolshevism swiftly and surely. Foch wanted a somewhat larger number of additional troops: 150,000, all of them volunteers.

Neither the British nor the American government was lacking in anti-Bolshevik sentiments. Lloyd George and Wilson spoke with deep aversion of the regime that had been established in Moscow. Nor had they any reason to assume that this regime was favourably disposed toward them. Since 1914, publicly and privately, Lenin had hurled unparalleled invectives against them. He laid down in black on white the international programme of a future Soviet government: "We would incite the proletariat of Europe to rebellion against its governments"—"We would rise against the remaining capitalist world, coming out, if necessary, even with armed force against the exploiting classes and their states." He had proclaimed the impossibility of any permanent compromise between the two systems. The capitalist states "can in no case and under no conditions live side by side with the Soviet Republic"—"the existence of the Soviet

Republic side by side with the imperialist states for an extended period is unthinkable."

He had even rejected the necessity of any economic collaboration with them: "They say we cannot get on without the financial support of England and France. But this supports us just as a noose 'supports' the man who is being hanged. Let the Russian revolutionary class say: Down with this support." These were declarations of war for the present and the future. The longing to see Lenin's creation perish was very strong in all the Allied chiefs.

Nevertheless the decision to change the anti-German intervention into an anti-Bolshevik one was not taken. Neither additional troops nor additional weapons were sent. The greatest reluctance to meddle in the struggle of the "Russian factions" prevailed. As Churchill wrote in several memoranda, there was "a complete lack of will to win"; a complete "lack of any genuine or effective effort to support the operations which are going on."

Instead, attempts were made to organize a kind of peace conference between the opposing Russian parties. These attempts failed; and when this solution proved impossible, the lack of will to win was openly transformed into the will to lose. In the fall of 1919 the months of irresolute delaying drew to a close; a decision was taken. It was the decision to quit Russia, to recall the few divisions and not to send any further aid to the anti-Bolshevik regimes. This decision amounted to yielding the victory within Russia to the Soviets, and in the course of the following two years the Bolshevik leaders did not fail to reap the fruits of this victory. From the point of view of the anti-Bolsheviks this capitulation was rather worse than the Munich pact of 1938 from the anti-Fascist point of view; and the consternation it evoked throughout the world was equally great. What remains of this story of Allied "intervention" is the fact that even under the conditions prevailing at that time both the United States and Great Britain shrank from waging an armed struggle against the Soviet regime. Not even when the Soviets were as good as defenceless could they resolve to wage such a struggle. They were not prepared to throw even another 150,000 men into it.

The co-existence of the Anglo-Saxon powers and the new Soviet state began with this most concrete illustration of the unwillingness of the former to apply armed force against the latter. It is natural to infer that this unwillingness must have grown ever more pronounced as Russia grew ever stronger. And this was so. In fact, during the next twenty years there was never a serious intention in England or the United States of breaking into Russia's house. True, the Russian government constantly sounded the alarm. For twenty years it kept saying that the victors of 1918 were preparing a war of annihilation against the Soviets. The accusation was directed now against England, now against America, now against France, finally even against the harmless League of Nations. But even those who let themselves be confused by the noise then will admit to-day in retrospect that all this talk was unjustified. England and the United States did not wish to fight Russia in 1919, when she was decimated and militarily defenceless; even less did they wish to fight her during the decades that followed, when she was gradually growing stronger and stronger. They will still less wish to fight her in the future, when she will enjoy greater military prestige than at any time since the days of Napoleon.

There may be friction, mutual irritation, blunders. These may have their causes in Moscow, London, or Washington. Annoyance, competition, differences of opinion and manœuvres, exist in every kind of relationship, and rarely through the guilt of only one of the parties concerned. But such details must be appraised against the background of the general character of a given policy. Whether the Secretary of State or the Under Secretary of State went to a conference, whether a passport was granted at once or after some delay, whether agreement in one case was not asked for and in another not given, such episodes, when they concerned Russia—and only when they concerned her—have been the occasion for extravagant interpretations. They did not deserve so much attention and never will. Even if the ultimate goals of a policy are not clear, the many negative little incidents that occur in every relationship cannot possibly be interpreted as so many symptoms of sinister intentions. England's and America's ultimate goals with regard to Russia have not been unclear. For the space of twenty years they wanted to be left in peace by her, and they wanted to leave her in peace. This attitude will be intensified in the future.

But what about Russia's attitude? Will she, too, desire only to be left alone by other states and to leave other states alone? If we come down to brass tacks, if we consider the situation in its essential features, what will take place among the big three will be determined by Russia, not by the others. It will depend upon whether Russia, too, assumes a conservative static international attitude; upon whether Russia, too, will wish to remain within the frontiers of her own immense empire, as it is absolutely certain the other two will do. Should this be her intention, peace will prevail between her and the two Anglo-Saxon powers. Any kind of friction among them will remain secondary and will be easily ironed out. But if Russia, in contrast to the two Anglo-Saxon powers, tries to reach out beyond her borders and increase her power, the horizon will darken. And let us not forget that power can have many forms and that various means can be used to attain it. Aside from territorial and military expansion there is spiritual or "ideological" expansion. We have discussed this subject before. There is no difference, except a quite irrelevant outward one, among the various forms which the expansion of power can assume. In any form it is a challenge. And we may add that it is a challenge no matter what the direction of the expansionist movement. Even a Russian expansion which would not aim directly at England and the United States would in the long run be just as inacceptable to these two powers as one aimed directly at them. It would be as inacceptable as Hitler's expansion was. He did not aim directly at England, either; he aimed at Austria, Czechoslovakia, and then Poland; and yet this expansion had to be stopped sooner or later. The eternal instinct of self-preservation inescapably demanded that it be stopped. Inescapably, the same instinct of self-preservation would operate again should Russia embark upon a policy of excessive expansion, no matter at whose cost. As things stand now, the future peace among the big three is in Russia's hands.

At present no one can foretell what direction Russia will take. The most important reason for our ignorance on this score is that probably no clear policy has as yet been formulated in Moscow itself. It is still too early. Doubtless there is a marked tendency toward expansion. And without doubt there are also strong factors working against this tendency. It is as good as certain that so far no decision has been made between the pros

5*

and the cons. The situation which will exist on the day of victory is still too uncertain. It is unpredictable where the various armies will be; what the domestic situation will be in all the countries involved; whether England's and America's determination will at that moment be strong and untrammelled or weak and war-weary. Stalin, who is praised for his realism, will not prematurely draw the balance of all the pros and cons. But the pros and cons are still there.

The pros are many. No one will deny that the Soviet regime came into the world with a frankly expansionist doctrine. It inherited this from Marx and even more from Lenin—Trotsky was only a minor apostle. This doctrine advocated the establishment of Communism in all the countries of the world; its establishment by force, for anything else, we were told, was inconceivable; and by the power of a domestic minority, plus Russian help, "even with armed force." This did not take place with the lightning speed Lenin expected in 1917. The strategy of reckless frontal offensives ended in failure everywhere. For this reason Lenin himself proclaimed a new kind of strategy, which was classically expounded in his book: *Left-Wing Communism: An Infantile Disorder*. The gist of this treatise was that we must adjust ourselves to a much longer waiting period. While we should be ready everywhere to start the attack at the right moment, we must in the meantime manœuvre with the maximum of resilience. We must have no prejudices against expedients of every conceivable sort. We must not shrink from temporary retreats, detours, camouflage, diversions, feints and shifts, pauses and armistices, which promise to be of any use. Thus the Bolshevik strategy was changed. Even under Lenin things were done which seemed completely incompatible with the original Marxian doctrine. In fact, from his time on, every outward congruence between what was done and what was taught practically disappeared. Nevertheless the aim remained unchanged. In so far as Lenin's doctrine is still accepted in Moscow to-day, it is a mighty argument for a post-war policy of expansion.

There are those who deny that Lenin's doctrines are still adhered to in Moscow. Trotsky maintained with rabid hatred and Mr. Joseph E. Davies maintains with admiring love that as far as Communist doctrine is concerned, Stalin is only a hypocrite, that at the bottom of his heart he long ago became an apostate. But it is impossible to accept this vilification of Stalin whether it is uttered in the language of hate or of love. There are no proofs; indeed, because of the nature of the question, there cannot be any proofs. The simple fact that Lenin sanctioned every detour, feint, and camouflage, even the most opportunistic ones, makes it impossible to prove that Stalin has forsaken his faith on any point. Everything that looks like apostasy may in reality be such a detour or feint and for that very reason be Leninist in the highest degree and consistent with a Communism free of "infantile disorders."

The concrete arguments that are supposed to prove Stalin's defection are extremely weak. Some go so far as to say that Communism in Russia has been abolished. To substantiate this assertion they cite the fact that incomes are no longer equal, but unequal, that there are fantastically high, medium, and miserably low incomes. They seem to forget that the essence of Communism is "the socialization of the means of production," which is fully in force in Russia. Not a single factory, bank, ship, or store is privately owned there. Therefore Communism exists in Russia. The salaries paid by the single employer, the state, are a minor matter. True, the original Communist doctrine regarded the equality of all incomes as one of the numerous subsidiary blessings which socialization would bring in its train. But it is not the only one of such subsidiary blessings which did not materialize—or have not yet materialized, Stalin might say— a temporary retreat in a minor field. Lenin made greater retreats than that.

Others make a point of Stalin's proclamation of "socialism in one country." This is supposed to run counter to Lenin's goal of socialism in all countries. The supporters and haters of his alleged betrayal declare that Stalin's thesis on the possibility of building Communism in Russia alone proves his lack of interest in Communism everywhere else. What an interpretation! As though my acceptance of one hundred dollars when I cannot get any more indicates a lack of interest in the thousand dollars I might get in the future. "Socialism in one country" means only one thing: if nothing better can be had, this will do. It never meant and never was supposed to mean: from now on we are not interested in anything more.

Still others claim to have discovered that Stalin is now a "Russian nationalist." This is supposed to imply a decisive break with the original Marxist-Leninist dogma. But here, too, we have an extremely uncertain argument. What we know is only that Stalin, in addition to the Communist ideology, has also made use of the nationalist one—just as now he seems to intend to mobilize even religion. It is true that, according to the orthodox philosophy, Communism and nationalism do not mix, that they are opposites. But practice and realism mock such theorizing. In the souls of simple Russian peasants, workers, and soldiers these two ideologies are juxtaposed and support each other. Toil, privation, and death are doubly glorified when they are made for the sake of both Communism, the liberator of peoples, and Little Mother Russia. At any rate, Communism and nationalism will not be in conflict as factors determining Russia's future international course. Every expansion of Communist Russia would be a gain for nationalist Russia, and every growth of nationalist Russia would widen the sphere of influence of Communist Russia. In this respect the two ideologies are completely identical. And even if Stalin became at the bottom of his heart exclusively nationalistic, he would still march into other countries under the flag of Communism. For this would secure for him in advance the support of considerable sections of the population. Napoleon, too, who was utterly indifferent to liberalism and democracy, did not invade any country under the slogan "France," let alone "Bonaparte," but under the slogan: *Liberté, Egalité, Fraternité*. This was half the secret of his success, as far as it went. Similarly, Russian nationalism and Communist ideology are not opposites; they complement each other and strengthen each other.

Then there is another argument in favour of expansion: opportunity. An opportunity that might be enormous in scope— an opportunity so unique that it might never occur again in Stalin's lifetime or after. In a military or spiritual or mixed form, expansion as far as the Atlantic and the Mediterranean and deep into Asia may become possible. It may happen that all Germany will fall under Russian or Communist domination—the goal of which Lenin dreamed, as Moses dreamed of the Promised Land. A German-Russian union would probably be able to gather to its standard all the rest of Europe without difficulty. But even without a detour via Germany the radius of conceivable possibilities encompasses all Europe. It reaches as far as China, Asia Minor and Persia. A host of possibilities for an immense Russian expansion through the power both of the sword and of the word will be provided in a world of mostly disarmed states; in a world of desolate and desperate states; of states with broken-down administrations and chaotic social organizations. This would be a bloc of about 550,000,000 people, not counting the colonies of the European countries. This would be by far the largest mass of completely civilized white people in the world and by far the greatest industrial potential in the world. It would be physically and psychically the most irresistible power in the world. The very uniqueness of such an opportunity will make it most tempting. The much more modest opportunities of 1939 and 1940 were exploited: the Red Army rolled across six frontiers.

But there are also strong arguments against the probability of Russian expansion. Russia is and will be for some time a gravely wounded country. Although from a purely military point of view her industry in the interior of the country has achieved remarkable results, the industry of western Russia is indispensable to Soviet economy—and this is in ruins. Cities lie in ruins, and the buildings and tools of several agricultural provinces have been destroyed. The people have lived through an inferno of blood-letting, of superhuman efforts and stark hunger. In this case it is not a cliché to say that after this war long years of peace and reconstruction will be the supreme need. Whether or not their leaders recognize this as the most essential need, they will certainly consider it an important element when weighing all the relevant factors in choosing a post-war course.

Furthermore, the opportunity to become established as a respected and feared partner in a triumvirate which will dominate the world is not one that presents itself every day. Co-operation and agreement with the two great Anglo-Saxon powers will bring about a state of affairs which will give the Russians not only great prestige but also more tangible advantages. These advantages will be most significant during the period of reconstruction: American and British contributions to this task can shorten it by years. But later, too, the partnership will bring all sorts of advantages. And all this will play its part in future decisions.

Finally there is the risk—implied in every expansionist policy—of an almost inescapable clash with those who could not possibly remain indifferent to the building up of an overwhelming and irresistible power. We know that through the two decades during which Stalin has guided Russia's foreign policy he has always displayed aversion to great risks. True, he tried many things, and nothing with success. From China in 1927 to Spain in 1936 he failed in everything he undertook. But he never undertook anything in such a fashion as to incur great risks. He never undertook anything that he could not drop at the first sign of failure. In 1939 and 1940, when for the first time he set his military machine in motion and marched into six countries, these moves involved no risk. And the greatest failure of his foreign policy resulted not from his having taken great risks, but from his attempt to avoid them: the fact that in 1941 and 1942 he was compelled to wage war alone was the result of his desire in 1939 to avoid waging war.

The risks of a great expansionist policy will weigh heavily with Stalin when the moment comes for him to make a decision. True, after the war extremely favourable conditions will be created for Russia; she will be the only great power on the continents of Europe and Asia—more than ever she will be the "bear" which will not be easily accessible to the "whale." She will have much greater prestige than before the war, and in every foreign country the phalange of her unreservedly devoted partisans will doubtless be more numerous than before. Even to-day there are in Moscow "free committees" for a number of countries, while "armies of liberation," "route armies," and the like function as Moscow's instruments in several lands. Nevertheless, the risk of a conflict with the two overseas mammoths remains the most dangerous of all conceivable risks, and will serve as the strongest counterweight against any expansionist tendencies.

Now, as this is being written, the pros and cons are obviously still being weighed. There is no doubt that Moscow is now engaged in sounding out how much Russian expansion the Allies will readily tolerate; and while trying to do this, it is also trying to increase this amount. Every visible sign fits into this pattern. As is usual in such cases, the system of the *douche écossaise* is in operation—an alternation of threatening groans and winning smiles. As usual, an artificial second front of diversions and compensations is being opened up; instead of the real question—Russian aspirations—public opinion hears constant and bitter complaints about all kinds of sins that are being committed against Russia. This method is particularly effective because of that strong element which, both in England and in the United States, is always unreservedly pro-Russian. Almost inevitably Washington and London will feel compelled to agree to a certain amount of Russian expansion. Only when the ultimate limit of their willingness to make concessions is established will Stalin enter upon the period of real decisions. And even then he may still await further developments.

One day, sooner or later, we shall know what his decision is. Anything that is said or written before that is irrelevant and insignificant. And let no one believe that there are powerful means of influencing this Russian decision. Tones, gestures, and minor details will hardly impress the realist without "infantile disorders." At bottom there is only the old, so very old question whether complaisance or intransigence is more effective. But whatever the answer, Russia's decision to expand or not to expand will determine her relations with her two great partners, and more than that: for all practical purposes, it will by itself determine the whole course of the world. It will be the crucial factor in shaping the future of mankind, the factor beside which all other so-called problems will seem bagatelles. In the last analysis, it is by this decision that the die of fate will be cast.

If the Soviets choose a static policy, no great storms are conceivable in our time after the elimination of Germany and Japan, for the few other nations who will be in a position to unleash such storms will not unleash them. The new era will be one of pacification, recovery, and peace. And while mankind, blissfully naïve, may regard such a state of affairs as natural, a small number will know that it is chiefly due to a difficult act of self-restraint on the part of Stalin. His credit in history will be great.

But should Stalin open the sluices of an expansionist policy—which would indeed be a disaster—there would be no preventative, no guarantee, no safety-valve, and no mechanism against its consequences. These consequences will have to be borne. The world would definitely not become collectively organized, but competitive and combative. Mankind will have to endure what it has endured for thousands of years. The great powers will manœuvre against one another, and in the end, unless a miracle intervenes, they will clash. We cannot know in advance which side will be victorious. In the past many an expansionist policy that seemed well conceived has had to be given up or has ended in crushing failure. The only protection against it was to be strong—a good idea in any case.

We can agree that *against wars among the big three no preventive means exists but their own will and self-restraint.*

Part Seven: Universal Democracy?

CHAPTER TWENTY

ON USING OPPORTUNITIES

MORE DRASTICALLY THAN any other events wars make us aware of the imperfections of our world and awaken in us an intense yearning to make it more perfect. To-day the air is heavy with this yearning. Strong is the desire, loud are the demands, numberless the ideas for changes and reforms.

There are changes and reforms which have something to do with the war, and there are others which have nothing to do with it. The distinction is clear enough. It is one thing to protect your house against dangers that threaten it from outside, such as storms and burglary and fire and explosions; it is another to improve and embellish it inside by making more satisfactory arrangements, installing more modern plumbing and more beautiful furniture. The former are related to the war; they are necessities made more acute by the war; the war itself urges and encourages us to satisfy them. The latter are completely unrelated to the war. No danger that threatens your house from outside is provoked by its inner defects, and no inner improvement contributes to repelling outside dangers. Ideas and plans of the first kind arise logically from the defects revealed by the war; they can be called the genuine peace and war aims. Ideas and plans of the other kind are brought into the discussion from quite different domains; they do not originate in the problems raised by the war and they have no bearing on these problems. They are superimposed war aims.

Popular feeling is little concerned with this distinction. For instance, there is the idea that the war must result in the improvement of low living standards where they exist. This is usually expressed less prosaically. Phrases like "the century of the common man," "the age of abundance," or "economic democracy" are preferred. But all these mean the same thing: that the living standards of the lower brackets must be raised. No other objective has been so fervently taken up as a war and peace aim as this one. Then there is something—not nearly so popular, but still strongly advocated—which could be called the pan-democratic objectives: the demand that the Allies concern themselves with establishing the democratic system in the defeated, liberated, and neutral countries all over the world. There is further the aim of the "people's revolution." This revolution is not defined very closely, but it goes without saying that it is only another name for what, in less discreet times, was called the "proletarian revolution."

Now, it must be granted that every kind of demand can be raised at any time. If the occasion presents itself, any cause can be connected with any other cause which really has nothing to do with it. The great peace settlement may very well have on its agenda other objectives in addition to the genuine war aims. And I am far from disputing in the least that some of the superimposed aims contain sympathetic and desirable elements. But it is necessary to present such plans and demands under their own colours. Yet consciously or unconsciously the colours usually get mixed up in the agitation. People do not say soberly: let us use this favourable opportunity to undertake this or that at the same time as we sign the peace; they say: this or that is inseparable from the peace, it is the very quintessence of all our war and peace problems. Let us reject this confusion.

It is a confusion deliberately fostered by those who intend to connect the war with a revolution. The idea is not new; it is Lenin's slogan: "Turn the imperialist war into a civil war!" all over again. The new circumstances have compelled a slight variation on the old theme. In 1917 Lenin issued appeals to the workers to make the revolution even during the war. The outcome of the war was a matter of indifference to him. To-day this indifference no longer exists; hence the revolution is not envisaged until after the war. But except for this small variation it is the same old thing. Only Lenin was frank enough to proclaim that the good opportunity must be used to "turn" the business of war into the completely different business of revolution. To-day's propaganda is trickier. According to it, these are not two completely different matters, and there is nothing to "turn" into something else. The people's revolution is already on the march: the war itself is the people's revolution. "This is not a war, this is a revolution." The revolution is presented as an aim which is inherent in the war. And if the war is the beginning of the revolution, what can its end be but the completion of the revolution? To think anything else would be a foolish rebellion against a decision already taken by history. We are advised to renounce futile resistance and voluntarily to open the door to the revolution so that it will enter with a friendlier countenance: "revolution by consent," as it has been called. Strong attempts were made to get the American and British governments to sponsor crypto-revolutionary measures in various countries, under the metaphysical pretext that the war, because it is a revolution, cannot be won in any other way.

Come, come—let us be intellectually honest. Let us not use words to mix things up instead of to clarify them. Let us not call a dictatorship a democracy; subjection, liberation; and war, a revolution. This war is a war. "The moon," says the neurotic Herod, "has a strange look to-night. She is like a madwoman, is she not?" "No," replies Herodias, "the moon is like the moon, that is all." The war is a war, that is all. Its meaning is that the Allied nations are fighting against other nations; its meaning is not, as in a revolution, that parts of the Allied nations are fighting one another. The cause of the war was that the Allied nations refused to be subjected by foreign rule, not that parts of the Allied nations wanted by force to impose new rulers upon themselves. There are two things involved here. There is the war; and as in every war and every peace, there is a certain amount of desire for revolution.

The number of those who are filled with this desire is probably larger in wartime than in the preceding period of peace— although no one really knows how large it is. But however large it may be, the war would still remain one thing and the revolution that is desired another. In the war no other war aims are inherent than those which are related to the prevention of new wars. Revolution is not a means for preventing wars—we have seen that before. It is a means to quite different ends. In my opinion it is a means to profoundly harmful ends. As Goethe said: "As much good is destroyed as is gained by it. I hate those who achieve it, as well as those who give cause for it." But even if the revolution served an eminently useful end, this end would still be essentially unrelated to the question of war and peace. The revolution is a superimposed war aim.

The case for the social reforms which are proclaimed as

essential to the conclusion of peace is similar. We welcome and support anything that can raise the living standards of the common man: but this again has nothing to do with the problems of war and peace. It is obviously absurd to include the social grievances of the American and British common man, whatever they may be, among the causes of the present war. It was not the British or American common people who wanted war because they lacked "abundance" or for other reasons. Nor did their lack of "abundance" attract the aggressor. And even if they lived amid the most overflowing abundance, it would not protect them from new aggressions. Actually, if one insists on explaining the war by a lack of abundance, only the lack of abundance among the common people of Germany and Japan could have caused it. Consequently, if we follow this idea to its logical conclusion, the most important task of the peace would be to raise the living standards not in the victorious countries but in the defeated enemy countries. This is the ironical result of connecting the war with the social problem. Fortunately, our conscience need not be exposed to this difficult test. The connection simply does not exist. We have investigated the "economic illusion" at length and need not repeat ourselves. It is quite clear that social magic, of whatever kind, cannot do away with wars. The aim of improving living standards is not inherent in the war itself. This aim, too, is a superimposed one.

Even the pan-democratic war aim, although not completely separate from the problems of war and peace, is only loosely connected with them. No one is more convinced than I that the democratic system—or, more accurately, the system of liberalism which in most cases is the substance of the democratic form—is the one most consistent with human dignity. No advantage offered by any other system is worth the hurt to human dignity which must be the price of such a system. But while there is every reason to cherish this immensely valuable aspect of democracy, we must not ascribe to it superiority in every domain. Although democracies go to war less easily than dictatorships, it remains true that democracies, too, have started wars. And it is also true that non-democracies have remained perfectly peaceful. For instance, dictatorial Turkey has not become involved in any war, and dictatorial Portugal has never shown the slightest aggressive tendency. From the point of view of international affairs there are various kinds of dictatorships: those in colossal states and those in unassuming little states; those with militaristic-expansionist features and those with distinctly static features. From the point of view of international peace every argument is in favour of preventively doing away with the dangerous kind of dictatorships as soon as possible. But from the same point of view the existence of small non-aggressive dictatorships is a matter of indifference. In brief, as far as peace is concerned, democracy is not always a guarantee and dictatorship is not always a fatality. The demand to establish democracy throughout the world touches the peace problem at certain points but does not coincide with it. Universal democracy without reservations is not a true war and peace aim. It, too, is a superimposed aim.

Naturally, the fact still remains that aims which have nothing to do with war and peace can be extremely desirable. Furthermore, even objectives which have nothing in common with one another can be achieved at the same time. It is nevertheless important that other aims, disguised as peace aims, be not smuggled into the peace discussions. An objective which is considered essential for the future peace is not the same thing as an objective to which such gigantic importance is not ascribed. Some burdens must be assumed in order to serve the cause of peace, and need not be taken up for other purposes. Certain risks must be accepted in one case and not in others. There are objections and scruples and refusals that in one case would constitute sabotage, and in another wisdom and caution. The difference between genuine and superimposed war aims is almost the difference between compulsion and free will. In one case we are under pressure; in the other we can choose.

There is another consideration that is not unimportant. In this war nations and armies are fighting for their very existence. A struggle for existence is not a minor matter. To preserve oneself, individually or collectively, is not an unimportant aim. It is incomparably the most important aim in this world. For this aim and no other, billions of people have sacrificed themselves and bled for thousands of years. For this aim, from the most ancient to the most recent times, people have fought against nature, wild beasts, and other people. This fight is none the less dignified because it guarantees only survival.

It is more than dubious whether in this war as in the last, it was wise to push the issue of self-preservation so far into the background as has been done—less in England than in the

United States. The belief that people suffer more willingly for shining ideals of future perfection and fight for them with greater enthusiasm than for the grim necessity of remaining alive seems to me to be based on rather artificial psychology. There are many arguments in favour of the contention that the naked truth—to wit, that this war is being waged simply in order not to be destroyed—is more inspiring and fortifying than all the complicated substitute aims. But let us at least be cautious about those substitute or superimposed aims which have no real prospect of being realized. For everything which is now declared to be the meaning and aim of this war is a promissory note that will be presented for payment the day after victory. Woe to the debtors if they are then insolvent. The result would be a new and perhaps worse repetition of the cynicism which spread over the world when the peoples realized that the brilliant promises of 1918 could not be made good.

We can agree—but can we?—that *we must distinguish carefully between genuine and superimposed war aims.*

CHAPTER TWENTY-ONE

AN EXCESSIVE BURDEN ON WEAK SHOULDERS

On the morrow of victory democracy will indisputably have won a triumph. It will have asserted itself in the United States and the British Commonwealth. Victory will mean that the heaviest assault made against democracy in all history has been crushed. This will be a tremendous achievement.

Furthermore, democracy will have a chance bordering on certainty in the liberated countries where it existed before and was defeated only by the force of foreign arms. For countries like Holland, Norway, Denmark, and even France and Belgium, the greatest optimism is justified. We have reason for hope even as regards the defeated countries. There is hope for Italy and for a garrisoned Germany. We shall leave prognostications about that great riddle, Japan, to others.

But these countries do not constitute the whole world. And they are in a special position. After the recession of the flood, new regimes will have to be organized there anyway, and Anglo-American troops will be present, at least at the beginning of these new regimes. But what about the rest of the world? Should we, of our own free will and in addition to our natural war aims, undertake to democratize the rest of the world?

Let us be frank and blunt. If the question is asked: Will all the countries, during the next few decades gradually introduce democracy, by themselves or, in the most extreme cases, with a little help?—we must answer: We don't know. We hope so. But this is not the idea that is being put forward. Translated from the language of enthusiasm into concrete terms, what is being put forward is the idea that the big three should set themselves up officially as the exterminators of every non-democracy in the world; that they should pledge themselves to the task of world-democratization; that they should undertake it systematically, as an integral part of their world policy; and that they should do this without delay. The same thing should be done, for the opposite purpose, as was done by the allied sovereigns after the Napoleonic Wars. Just as they solemnly pledged themselves in 1815 to defend monarchic legitimacy all over Europe and to prevent the establishment of new democracies, the Allies of today are asked to pledge themselves to eliminate all the dictatorships in the world and permit only democracies to exist. My contention is that anything even approximating this idea is absolutely inconceivable. To say this is not pleasant for anyone who feels the most violent aversion to every kind of non-democracy. It is a truth to which we can resign ourselves only with difficulty. But it is a truth. The idea of imposing world democracy is an attractive illusion, but it is an illusion.

Anyone who thinks through this idea in a down-to-earth fashion comes up once more against the special nature of our Russian ally. Once again we are confronted by the fact that Russia is not a democracy. She is anything but that, and the recently adopted practice of applying the adjective "democratic" to the Russian system does not change the fact. The decision to call a circle a square may after some time lead to a situation in which many people will not know the meaning of the words "round" and "square." But by whatever name we call a circle, it remains a circle. Even when she is called "democratic," Russia remains the very opposite of a democracy. All the maxims and institutions and processes which constitute the criteria of a democracy are in Russia replaced by other and opposite maxims, institutions, and processes. Thus we are confronted by the question: How could a policy of world democratization be carried out by the common efforts of the big three?

It is impossible even to imagine. It is simply impossible that Moscow's ideas of the institutions to be set up anywhere, of the persons to be entrusted with the task, of the course to be followed by them, could ever coincide with London's and Washington's ideas on the same questions. In fact, we run into the discovery that we made earlier when we discussed the re-education of Germany: there is a limit to all collaboration between the West and Soviet Russia, and this limit begins in the domain of ideology. Let me repeat what I said then: It is not true that ideological discrepancies between Russia and her Anglo-American Allies must necessarily prevent every common practical undertaking. Far from it. Common action in all matters of power politics are possible; and the preservation of peace by authority is a form of power politics. Agreement on all technical procedures and measures is possible. But just as a common democratic indoctrination of children is impossible, so democratic reorganization of other countries undertaken in common is impossible. Whenever the question of a new regime comes up for any country, the ideas of the Russians will in all human probability always be in opposition to the ideas of the English and Americans. It is possible that this opposition will not be revealed at the first stage of a transformation, but only at its second or third stage. But it is quite clear that in these matters the long-range ideas of Russia and the Allies are not identical, but profoundly different. There is no real basis for co-operation in the process of democratizing the world. The most optimistic prospect is that Russia will keep out of this field, that she will leave it to England and the United States and that she will remain neutral in matters concerning the democratization of other countries. Then the burden would lie not on three nations, but on two. Pan-democratization would have to be carried out by the power of the two Anglo-Saxon commonwealths alone. Such is the first observation we must make, even in the most optimistic case.

But this is only the prologue to the drama. The first act begins when we start to look at the countries in which the mission of democratization would have to be carried out. The sad truth is that, aside from the United States and the British Commonwealth, there are at present practically no democracies left. Expressed in figures: outside the two Anglo-Saxon countries there are about 1,500,000,000 people, of whom at present not even 50,000,000 are organized democratically. Only little Sweden and littler Switzerland are still genuinely democratic. Even if we generously include a few small South American republics, there remain about 1,450,000,000 people living in several dozen states who are not democratized. Among these are the 300,000,000 Germans, satellites, and their victims who will in any case be the responsibility of the Allies, and the 100,000,000 Japanese and Koreans. Whether they like it or not, the British Commonwealth and the United States will have to assume certain tasks in connection with the establishment of new regimes in the states of these 400,000,000 peoples. But there remains a mass of about 1,050,000,000 non-democratically ruled people, and a policy of world democratization would have to accept this burden and responsibility of its own volition. Thus two Commonwealths of less than 200,000,000 white inhabitants would be burdened with the political future of 400,000,000 plus 1,050,000,000 foreign people.

There is an especially paradoxical element in this situation. These non-democracies consist not only of neutrals like Argentina, Spain, and Turkey; a considerable number of them are Allies! For it is a truth that while in one respect this complicated war is clearly enough a war of democracies against autocracies, it is in other respects a war between autocracies. We no longer live in the simpler world of 1914. The Allies no longer constitute the camp of the democracies, with Czarist Russia as the only great exception. Since then the world has degenerated. The democracies have become fewer. In the camp of the Allies of to-day the democracies are a minority and the non-democracies a majority. By no stretch of the imagination can Chiang Kai-shek's China be called a democracy. Nor Stalin's Russia, nor Varga's Brazil, nor Salazar's Portugal. They are dictatorships— of various shades, but dictatorships none the less. A minority of the Allies are trying to win this war in order to preserve their democracies. But a majority of them are trying to win this war in order to preserve their dictatorships. The common victory will be not only a victory for the democratic system, but just as much a victory for the dictatorial system.

Thus the proponents of world democratization are from the

very first faced with a hopeless dilemma. No normal human being harbours the notion that after the war the United States and England should undertake to overthrow the Russian and Chinese regimes. That idea is so absurd that no more words need be wasted discussing it. But if world democratization must omit Russia and China, one can no longer speak of world democratization. The mission of democratization would be for all practical purposes limited to only a part of the world. The principle would be gone, and with it its magic and justification. In fact, if the most important dictatorships must remain what they are, why accept the burden of changing the less important ones? If not Russia and China, why Brazil? And if not the Allies, why the neutrals? If not Brazil, why Spain and Turkey?

But there is something else which is even more important from a practical point of view. No one can imagine that for the peoples of the United States and the British Commonwealth democracy in foreign countries is so important that they will voluntarily make continual sacrifices for its sake. And such sacrifices would be necessary. An Anglo-American policy of democratization would step into all the hornets' nests of the world. It would create disturbances and turmoil in many corners and these would have to be dealt with. To impose the will of the greatest countries even on the smallest, some form of power is required—and the spiritual form of power by itself would not get very far in the dictatorships. Trade wars and naval demonstrations and occupations of territory and direct or indirect participation in civil wars would be required. Who can seriously believe that the English and American politicians and parties and public would agree to all that for any period of time only in order to secure the triumph of democracy in foreign countries?

As a matter of fact, we have convincing proofs to the contrary. Democracy has not proved itself a suitable instrument for spreading democracy. One democracy after another was destroyed without a majority in the other democratic nations insisting that this process be prevented by armed intervention. On the contrary, we saw that the overwhelming majority was willing, for the sake of its own tranquillity, even to be party to this destruction. This was most clearly demonstrated in the case of Czechoslovakia. Yes, in Munich it was not only territories that were handed over to Germany. Lord Runciman's report on which the deal was based said explicitly that in the rest of Czechoslovakia the internal regime would have to be adjusted to the German pattern—and let no one say that the Munich agreement was disapproved by the English people. They approved it even with this condition. Nor did the present war originate in the desire of the Anglo-Saxon nations to save democracy in foreign countries. They wanted to save the framework of their accustomed way of life in their own countries and for themselves.

The belief that all the peoples are ready for a policy of world democratization is a beautiful dream, but it is only a dream. It would be pure fantasy to put a policy of this kind on the official Anglo-American programme. The Holy Alliance of 1815 was capable of fulfilling the mission of universal anti-democracy only for a few years. In 1822, when Ferdinand of Spain was captured and imprisoned by the rebels, and France, acting as plenipotentiary for the Holy Alliance, restored legitimacy with her troops, it was the swan-song of the Alliance. It was its last "intervention." And then the situation was relatively simple. The Allies of that time were absolutist sovereigns; they did not have to worry much about parties and public opinion. To-day, in countries with parties and legal oppositions, a reversed Holy Alliance would be all the more shortlived. It is almost a hundred per cent. certain that after two or three years at most public opinion and the political bodies would no longer play the game. A government that was willing to enter upon this path of constant vexations would be prevented from continuing on it. The attempt would end ingloriously in hypocrisy and demoralization—and a considerable amount of unfinished business in various corners of the world.

This is mankind as it is, not as it should be. This is the real mankind, the old Adam. We must yield to the properties of the "material with which we must build." We shall be lucky enough if the old Adam in the United States and the British Commonwealth persists in the three urgent tasks he has. These three tasks are: to democratize the defeated countries to some extent, to help the liberated nations resurrect their democracy, and to intervene in time against those dictatorships which, as a result of their size and militaristic features, gravely imperil the peace. Even this is a big programme. Even this presupposes a great deal of perseverance, far-sightedness, and willingness to make sacrifices, as well as a good memory. But to extend this programme to include all mankind would be an excursion into unreality.

This does not imply that the opposite of a programme of world democratization should be advocated. The impossibility of attempting to do something everywhere and under all circumstances does not mean that we should never attempt it under any circumstances. Here, as in so many questions of international politics, Talleyrand's maxim: "The best principle is to have none," is not cynical, but wise. Here, as everywhere else, Bismarck's definition that politics is "the art of the possible" is valid. What is impossible as a programme for all times and all places may be possible in individual cases at definite times. Here or there the position of some Franco may become shaky. Here or there a new democracy may become ripe for birth. There may be cases in which not much outside aid would be required to secure a happy ending to these eventualities. A minimum of pressure on the one hand and a minimum of support on the other may suffice to topple the balance. Even should more be required, the President and the Prime Minister of to-morrow may find that in a certain specific case public opinion is behind them even if larger-scale actions are necessary. Let us hope that such cases will be numerous. Let us hope that they will be handled in the right way. But this is something different from a doctrine, from a settled universal policy, from a solemnly signed Holy Alliance of Pan-Democracy.

We can agree that *the establishment and preservation of universal democracy is a task beyond the strength of the Allies.*

CHAPTER TWENTY-TWO

THE FRUITS OF VICTORY
AND THE STORM

ASK TEN MEN what things they demand above all from their statesmen the day after victory, and seven or eight, almost without thinking, will mention the superimposed social objectives we have discussed above. Even before they speak of the peace itself they will come forth with some formulation which expresses the hope of improved living standards for the little man. And let us add that what they hope for is not a gradual, step-by-step improvement. They expect extraordinary, sudden, and revolutionary improvements. More or less clearly defined measures from above are demanded, novel, fundamental, epoch-making measures.

This expectation is so strong that it will surely take the form of a political movement initiated the moment the last shot is fired—at the very latest. Even now, while the war is still on, the outbreak of such a movement is being prevented only with difficulty. Immediately after the war the leaders will open the sluices. The flood of popular desire will rush forward and seek with ever increasing energy to find its path. It will be of little use to stand up and cry: "Stop! This is a mistake! This has nothing to do with the real problems of peace!" The movement will not listen to the truth, however important it may be, that the peace should be given precedence. It will not keep in the background until the problems of the peace are solved. On the contrary, it will try to present its demands as an integral part of the peace problem. It seems beyond doubt that, at the very moment the international settlement will have to be made, a social movement will arise which has no connection with this settlement, but which will be none the less stormy and intense.

The prospect of this simultaneity is most disquieting. For there is a great danger that the work of making the peace will be very much disturbed, if not completely ruined, by the outbreak of social conflicts.

And they will indeed be sharp conflicts. It would be naïve

to imagine that the social movement will achieve its aims smoothly. Few things will be achieved "by consent"—not even things which are far from revolutionary. Proposals for raising the standard of living of those in the lower brackets soon reach a point at which no consent can be expected. The situation will be different in different countries. But in America, for instance, no consent can be expected for measures which would imply new breaches in the capitalist system, the system of free enterprise. Should the demands be in this direction—and that is what is usually meant by epoch-making measures—more stubborn resistance is to be expected than at any time since the great depression. Nor can it be expected that the hoped-for, extraordinary, sudden, and revolutionary improvements will materialize. In fact, it cannot be expected that any measures whatsoever, of whatever nature, could fulfil the hopes that are now entertained. Under any circumstances the results will fall considerably short of what man's fantasy has promised him. For this reason it must be assumed that the violence of the movement will only grow for some time. In brief, conflicts are to be expected; conflicts which will grow increasingly bitter and turbulent for a few years, until a decision is reached or weariness sets in. To imagine anything else is to indulge in wishful thinking.

Now, for ninety-nine per cent. of the people domestic struggles are incomparably more important than foreign affairs. Bismarck preached the "primary of foreign politics," but he preached it to deaf peoples and politicians. We have seen often enough how thoughtlessly and even unscrupulously the most important foreign-political objectives were sold for a domestic mess of pottage. According to the famous law of Gresham, bad money always displaces good money; similarly there seems to be a law according to which in times of conflict domestic interests always displace foreign-political interests. The shirt is closer to the skin than the coat. The domestic enemy is the familiar Mr. X and the familiar group Y, and what is in dispute is the familiar issue Z. Such stakes arouse men to the point of frenzy. Foreign politics, world politics—these mean remote peoples and dull, complicated issues. They are not half so exciting as domestic struggles. This creates a disturbing outlook in a situation in which the peace settlement will have to be made at the very moment that a bitter social struggle begins.

It is well to realize this danger clearly. The work of the peace conference will certainly not be helped by grave domestic struggles being fought out behind its back. Such struggles tend to cripple the government involved at the negotiation table. It will lack the energy and strength, the peace of mind and self-assurance that are required in this business. True, such a situation threatens only England and the United States, not Russia. The Russians will not have social conflicts at their rear. But for the Russians, too, another danger is important: the danger that, as a result of these struggles in other countries, all the international fronts will be shifted and muddled. The movement will sweep all the countries with varying strength and varying results. In one country one party will be successful, in another country another. And naturally the two camps in every country will co-operate with the related camps in every other country. The related camps will try to support one another and obtain support from one another. This will bring completely new affinities and groupings into the international picture. Every country in which the Left wins the upper hand will be a protector and protégé of the Leftists in all the other countries. Likewise, every Right will help and receive help from the countries in which the Rightists are victorious. Call this an international class struggle or what you will: it must result in the tendency to bury all the interests and ideas inherent in this war under new, quite different ones, and to discard all the partnerships necessary for the peace in favour of hectic casual flirtations.

The possible situations that may result from the confusions and dislocations brought about by acute social struggles defy the imagination. To quote only two examples among hundreds, a Germany cleverly groomed to look Leftist might become a vehemently defended fellow traveller of an England drifting Leftward; or a Germany cleverly rigged out on a Rightist model might become a favoured junior partner of an America drifting Rightward. And so on through the entire gamut of objectives and problems and participants. Should the social struggle reach white heat, may God have mercy on the work of the peace settlement!

Unfortunately, it must be repeated, even these threatening prospects will probably not act as a deterrent. Although they are threatening for all sides, the outbreak of the social movement will not for this reason be postponed until after the peace settlement. Since this is so, it seems necessary to hasten the conclusion of the peace before the social movement gets into high gear.

This is the first almost certain inference to be drawn from the luxuriant growth of superimposed war aims.

It is well known that some people advise the exact opposite: they want the war to be followed by a long "cooling off" period or a "long armistice" and to make the actual settlement only "when things can be seen more clearly." This proposal has met with much applause, which is understandable if only because it grants a most welcome moratorium to helplessness. And this is not the only merit of the proposal. Other reasons, too, can be advanced in favour of a "cooling off" period—provided a cooling off is really in prospect. But the truth is that in one important respect we must look forward not to a cooling off but to a warming up. And so what is necessary is speed. When rain and storms threaten, farmers bring the harvest into the barns as fast as they can. There are urgent reasons for bringing the harvest of victory into the barn as fast as possible before the social movements and counter-movements assume large proportions. Once they have reached large proportions—which is not a certainty, but a possibility—there will be danger of a displacement of the fronts and a dislocation of all relationships. Then no one will any longer know who is and will be for or against anything. The work of the peace settlement might suffer incalculable damage, not only because the peace problems themselves would become more controversial, but because they would become a ring in which conflicts of a completely different kind and origin would be fought out. Unsettled questions are always the most favourable soil on which conflicts are fought out. If the social struggles reach their climax only after the peace has been written, the latter will not be essentially affected by the former. If the peace settlement has not yet been made, it will become the chief battleground of the social issues. Then it may become actually impossible to make a peace settlement which corresponds to the victory and deserves its name.

One cannot see who would gain from taking such incalculable chances. No one can prophesy what course the social movement will take. In the presence of such threats we should assume that all the parties involved have an equal interest in making the settlement as speedily as possible.

We can agree that *superimposed social objectives make violent internal conflicts almost certain. The conclusion of peace should be so speedy that it is not affected by the confusion inherent in such conflicts.*

CHAPTER TWENTY-THREE

OUR COURSE AT THE SOCIAL CROSSROADS

IN 1800 A BRICKLAYER in London earned about nineteen shillings a week. Before the first World War this amount rose to forty-seven shillings. Before the last depression it had risen to seventy-seven shillings. And after a temporary drop, it reached the same figure before the outbreak of the second World War. During all this period the London bricklayer's income increased considerably; the statistical records bear witness to the fact that the common man did not have a bad century.

Once at his new level, the bricklayer naturally still had unsatisfied desires. Neither objectively nor, above all, subjectively, was he sated. This is the nature of man. What has been achieved is taken for granted, and what has not yet been achieved is demanded. What is called progress is founded on this human trait. But in the century behind us enormous progress was made. In truth, although it was not so called, it was the century of the common man *par excellence*—the best that he had ever had. In the days of Jefferson, Napoleon, and Pitt the living standards in the lower brackets were actually about the same as in the days of Columbus and Cromwell; they had remained practically unchanged since the Middle Ages. Then in one single century they rose more than in all the preceding centuries combined. And this not only in England, but everywhere else; and not only in the bricklayer's trade but in all the trades, or, more accurately, in all the categories of labour. The pace of development was not quite so rapid in other occupational categories.

Yes, the common man, especially the worker, rose mightily as regards income and consumption. Although in 1800 the shilling and the dollar could in many respects buy more than they can to-day, they bought considerably less in other respects. While most foodstuffs were cheaper then, most industrial goods are cheaper—unimaginably cheaper—to-day. Wages rose not only in dollars and pounds sterling, but also in real purchasing power. And the rate of increase grew as time went on. During the fifteen years from 1914 to the great depression alone, the average wage of the industrial worker, according to American statistics,

6

increased by thirty-two per cent in terms of purchasing power. No less eloquent is the enormous *per capita* rise in production, importation, and consumption that took place in this century, not to speak of the tremendous increase in the variety of goods. In the main, it was the household of the common man that absorbed all these increases. During this period he attained a standard of income and consumption of which he had not even dreamed in 1800.

Nor was this all. During the same period the amount of labour he had to expend decreased steadily. The memory of the starting-point of this march forward does not seem to be very much alive, and the appreciation of what has been attained is inadequate. But one fact will perhaps make it clear to us. Into a world which formerly had not been in the least concerned with the limitation of working hours came the English factory law of 1833. At first it ventured to attack only one kind of labour: child labour. The humanitarian maximum established was: for children under thirteen years of age, nine hours a day; for children between thirteen and eighteen, twelve hours a day. The grown-ups worked fourteen hours and more. Such was the state of affairs at that time. But in the course of the century child labour disappeared almost entirely. By 1918, most adults in all civilized countries had attained the eight-hour day, and in 1939 had reached the forty-hour week. And it is impossible to compare the difficulty of labour to-day with that of a century ago.

It is important to recall that precisely in this field Karl Marx's "inexorable laws" were most inexorably demolished. For with the most vehement assurance Karl Marx had prophesied the exactly opposite development. Under the capitalist system, he taught, it was unavoidable that wages should deteriorate constantly and hours of labour grow steadily longer. This is the famous "theory of increasing misery," to which so many weighty pages are devoted in *Capital*, particularly in the great forecast of developments in Chapter xxv: "Within the capitalist system all methods for raising the social productiveness of labour are brought about at the cost of the individual labourer. It follows that in proportion as capital accumulates, the lot of the labourer must grow worse. Accumulation of wealth at one pole is accumulation of misery, agony of toil, slavery, ignorance, brutality, mental degradation at the opposite pole. As means are constantly being found for the maintenance of labour on cheaper and more wretched food, the minimum of wages is constantly sinking."

Decade after decade the master's companions-in-arms and disciples waited for that worsening of wages and lengthening of the working day which had been scientifically forecast. At every temporary setback in the real development which so obviously contradicted this forecast, they thought: "Now it is beginning!" When it never began, they gradually acknowledged that in this single prognosis the master had been mistaken. But, they said, this one mistake does not matter; the doctrine as a whole still remains valid. They overlooked the fact that the "theory of increasing misery" is not a detail, but the pillar on which the whole doctrine of the desirability and inevitability of socialism rests. According to this theory, only because capitalism is unable to lead to anything but declining wages and increasing working hours is it a curse for mankind and for itself; a thing doomed to destroy itself; a thing whose existence is one single continuous suicide.

It is important to recall this, for it has an essential bearing upon the question whether social progress can be achieved only by changing the economic system itself. Immense social progress has been achieved within this system. To be sure, it has not been achieved because the managers of the system pursued this objective. The capitalists' motive was not to achieve social progress, but to earn profits and be successful. In pursuing this motive they displayed the same average degree of stupidity, selfishness, and wickedness as all classes of the human race in any of their affairs, and sometimes possibly even more. Much had to be wrested from them by social struggles and political coercion. But even more was accomplished automatically, without extraneous intervention: through the reduction of production costs, new inventions, effects of competition, and so on. This was the way in which the capitalist system worked. By its own inner movement, implemented by its characteristic political institutions, it produced social progress unprecedented in extent and tempo. "The century of the common man" is nothing new in this world. What can be demanded is really only a second century of the common man. And the second would not have to be called bad if it brought results similar to those of the first. If at its end the London bricklayers and all their fellow-workers have once again multiplied their present income and seen their working hours reduced by half—well, in A.D. 2000 this again will certainly not be regarded as "abundance." But in the light of present-day ideas it would be a fantastic amount of abundance!

Very well, then, if the system once was able to produce such results, why should it not be able to do it again? This question leads us to a striking discovery. It turns out that in recent times the social movements of all colours have changed their flags. Without exception they have replaced their old demands and arguments by new ones. These are no longer concentrated on the lot of those who work, but on the lot of those who do not work.

For many decades the alpha and omega of every variety of social reformism was the common working man, the working proletarian. It was from his situation that the necessity of great evolutions or revolutions was deduced. These evolutions or revolutions were designed to improve his position. The existence of a bottom layer of unemployed was naturally mentioned. Marx called it the "industrial reserve army." But to some extent he did not even consider the condition of this layer of people a subject worth discussing. The subject to which he devoted pages and chapters was the present and still worse future misery of the people who had jobs. His successors did the same thing, as well as the representatives of all other tendencies of social critique. In time the misery of the worker grew less and less impressive, and the professional critics took increasingly dubious brands of misery as their theme. During the 1920s, for instance, the favourite theme was the sufferings caused by the conveyor belt with its nerve-shattering uniformity. The workers themselves seemed to prefer the conveyor belt to older methods. But the object of the social movement was still the worker who had a job.

Came the great depression of the thirties, with the worst attack of unemployment that had ever been seen. As we know, this scandalous event had many consequences, not the least important of which was the sudden great shift of the social demands and arguments from the worker who had a job to the worker who had none. "Decrepit capitalism!" cried the Communists; "in Soviet Russia there is no unemployment!" "Decadent plutocracies!" cried the Nazis; "in Germany there is no unemployment!" Consternation seized the world, it was swept by a *grand'peur* as in the Middle Ages. The trauma of unemployment remained deep in men's minds, and dominated all debates and popular agitation. And since that time social demands have no longer been supported by arguments relevant to the employed workers, but to the unemployed. Social demands no longer take the normal regular situation of the overwhelming majority into account, but the abnormal temporary situation of a minority. It is no longer the lot of most of the people all of the time that is made into the social criterion, but the lot of some of the people some of the time.

The consequences of this shift are tremendous, for it leads us from a domain in which the record of the capitalist system is really good into one in which it is indubitably bad. For all common people with jobs the capitalist system has been demonstrably lucrative. But just as demonstrably the capitalist system is unable always to give employment to all common people. Thus different conclusions are reached, according to the point at which the social demands are focussed. Is it demanded that the standard of the employed be further improved? Then it would be absurd to abolish capitalism. Or is it demanded that everyone at all times should be employed? Then it is absurd to retain the capitalist system.

Such are the sober facts. In the course of its great march forward the capitalist system has brought a constant and enormous increase in well-being for all who were employed under it. There is no serious reason to expect a richer economic yield for the working man from any other system, not to mention a noneconomic yield which is even more important: the political yield. But there is no use quibbling about the fact that under capitalism temporary unemployment is inevitable. The depressions which take place at intervals of from seven to ten years are just as inherent in the mechanism of the system as are the booms. They are a function of the famous "automatism" which regulates the system. Because of this automatism they are inevitable and necessary, just as it is inevitable and necessary for the human organism not only to breathe in, but also to breathe out; not only to eat, but also to eliminate wastes.

There are means of making depressions milder and shorter than was the scandalous depression of the thirties. There are means of providing much better assistance to their temporary victims. I shall speak about these later. But within the capitalist system there are no means of eliminating depressions; hence there are no means of eliminating a certain amount of unemployment during a certain period of time. Those who promise the opposite promise something which cannot be realized. Thus the social problem confronts us with an alternative that should not be veiled, but should, on the contrary, be made as clear as possible. Shall we steer our course with our eyes on the employed or the unemployed? Shall the pole of our compass be the ordinary situation of the majority or the extraordinary situation of the minority? Most of the people all of the time or some of the people some of the time—that is the question.

We know from experience that at a certain point in any discussion of the social problem all agreement ends. But it should still be possible to agree that *the capitalist system was and is able constantly to improve the standard of the employed common man. It was and is unable constantly to employ every common man.*

CHAPTER TWENTY-FOUR

UNEMPLOYMENT UNDER CAPITALISM

CAPITALIST ECONOMY cannot guarantee jobs to all the people at all times. But even without changing this economy two important goals can be achieved. The negative business cycle need not be nearly as negative as it was in the sinister thirties; and greater protection can be given those who are nevertheless uprooted by depressions. Let us see here to what extent the capitalist system itself provides means of conquering the plague of unemployment.

One fact of general significance must be stated at the outset: the capitalist system can reveal its best qualities only under conditions of a stable peace. This may sound somewhat trivial, but it is anything but that. It is a fact of the most concrete and paramount importance. For it explains why the depression of the thirties was so much more violent than all previous depressions: the world was not in a state of peace; for about nine years it had been engaged in a constant, ever more tormenting death struggle of the peace. Because of this murderous political state of affairs, the depression was prevented from taking a normal course.

Yes, the black plague of the thirties was in fact caused by two entirely separate phenomena which happened to coincide. One was the crash of 1929, which followed a period of wild prosperity with the usual consequences. These consequences were in no way

different from what had taken place in 1907, 1900, or 1890.
Nothing inherent in the process itself called for a development
different from the usual one; that is, after the crisis a period of
liquidation; then two or three years of depression; finally a new
upswing. But beginning in 1930 another element was added to
the situation. Unlike what had taken place in all previous cases,
the economic depression was complicated by a political world
crisis. Europe and Asia began to smoulder. The stench of powder
and dynamite rose like an ever thickening cloud. This was what
prevented the normal reascent from the depression to a new
boom. The absence of peace, the imminence of war, throttled
the normal capitalist mechanism.

At the time, this state of affairs was not understood. In fact,
throughout the two "accursed decades," as I have called them,
very little of what was happening was understood. There has
always been much justification for a gloomy view of the capacity
of human reason. "There is no parallelism between the development of science and the development of the mind," said Clemenceau. "Human beings are like apes who have stolen Jupiter's
thunder." But the agitation and discussion dealing with the great
depression are perhaps the most incriminating evidence ever
produced against human reason. As though everything was not
within the hand's grasp! According to the normal development
of business cycles the new upward trend after a depression begins
with a rise in investments. The capitalists who have hitherto
feared losses everywhere begin again to feel optimistic and
instead of thinking only of the best means of preserving their
capital think again of profits. Whereas until this moment, anxious
for the security of their money, they have not only failed to invest
in new enterprises, but also reduced and liquidated the old
ones wherever possible, they now consider conditions as again
secure enough to risk a little here and there. The "strike of the
capitalists" ebbs and gradually a new boom develops.

Can there be any doubt why this feeling of security could
not develop in the thirties? Was it not clear why after each short
flickering it was immediately quenched again? As early as 1930
Hitler's first enormous electoral success announced the collapse
of the Versailles peace. In 1931 came the grave international
convulsion that resulted from the first German attempt at a
veiled "Anschluss" with Austria. In the same year Japan jumped
at China's throat, and all hope of achieving peace by collective

security vanished. In 1933 Hitler acceded to power and German rearmament began. In 1934—but why continue to recapitulate? The dogs of war could be clearly heard running from all corners of the planet. How could a new feeling of confidence and optimism arise in investors and capitalists? Who wants to invest in business which may to-morrow be stopped or destroyed by war? A heavy boot trampled upon the field and squashed the cabbage heads. The following morning the experts came and with their magnifying glasses and balances and retorts investigated why the plants were growing so badly. "A miserable seed was used, from which, naturally, nothing can grow," said one expert. "No, this soil is deadly for vegetables, as I have always shown," said another. "Nonsense, it's the fertilizer, which should have been improved," said a third. The following night the boot again trampled upon the cabbages. And the gentlemen went on disputing over the seeds and the soil and the fertilizer.

There is nothing sadder than the library of scholarly and propagandist works which were written about the last depression, its gravity and length. Their only value is that of another monument to a period which simply could not understand itself. That it did not understand itself politically is indisputable to-day. We know the consequences of the fact that for ten years the war was allowed to prepare itself, to spread and to deepen. We know what we owe to the inaction and blindness and cowardly hush-hush tactics of the rulers and the ruled, to the amateur snake-charmers of business as usual, wages as usual, and politics as usual, who with rare unanimity prevented the abscess from being cauterized soon enough. But it is high time we realized that we owe to the same policy the economic disaster of this period: the extraordinary length and gravity of the depression. Neither the economic system nor economic policies were responsible for this. Neither less nor more of a New Deal could have helped. The depression was bound to be endless and abysmal because capitalist economy simply cannot function without security and stability. The depression of the thirties would have been an ordinary depression if the world had been at peace. This explains the misery we experienced; and this can also free us from the traumatic shock caused by that misery. There is no need to fear the return of a black plague of such violence and stubbornness! There will be no repetition of it if a stable peace prevails on earth. So let us not indulge in excessive fears. The emergencies we must expect after the era of economic demobilization — which, it is true, will last for some time—are only the emergencies of normal depressions.

Is there a possibility of alleviating these too? There certainly is.

To-day, of course, the capitalist system exists only in theory; the war has suspended it. But even before the war it had been brought to a pass in which it was unable to reveal its best qualities. In more than one respect it had become a mutilated system, an amphibious system—if one may apply the term "amphibious" to a fish with half its fins cut off and replaced by legs, a fish that can no longer swim properly, and yet cannot run properly. Not a very happy condition.

A definitely unpopular subject must be taken up at this point: the subject of profits. Whoever discusses it exposes himself deliberately to hostile reactions. He risks incurring the enmity of moralists whose economic ideals seem to be a kind of immaculate conception. In matters of biology it would be rather futile to advocate this sinless method of procreation, although some austere temperaments seem to be inclined to do even that. But in economic matters the fact that procreation is induced by the sinful urge for profits is widely disapproved. The investor who is motivated by this low aim is not treated with consideration. The tendency to deprive him of the largest part of his profits through taxation is widespread. Nevertheless, the capitalist system cannot afford to let this policy be pushed too far.

For there is only one single fuel that sets the motor of capitalist economy in motion and keeps it going: profit. This is the blunt truth. A factory is founded for no other motive than to make profit; it is not founded if the possible profit in it does not counterbalance the risks of capital loss and profitless years.

Now, there is little doubt that the taxation of profits overstepped the optimum in most countries even before the war. This alone impaired the operation of the capitalist system. The idea underlying the excessive taxation of profits was less fiscal than ethical: it was the ideal of equalization. But the capitalist system is frankly an opportunistic, not an ethical system. Equality is definitely antipathetic to it. Equality spells the death of its mechanism. It is questionable whether even socialism is different in this respect. It was not because of a whim that Russia returned from the ethics of equality to the opportunism of colossal inequality. At any rate, too much equality is something that does not fit

6*

very well into the capitalist system; and in its complex "dialectics" those who suffer from excessive equality are not so much the rich as the poor. The millionaires are not to be pitied; they still fare well enough. Their complaints about being bled white are boring, if not repulsive. But the consequences for the plain people are serious. Too much taxation of the few millionaires means in prosaic reality too few new jobs for the innumerable common people.

There is even a worse obstacle to the best working of the system—and here the capitalists themselves are for the most part responsible. They themselves have destroyed one of the most essential conditions for the functioning of capitalism. These traitors to their own system, out of blindness or narrow-minded personal interest, have destroyed what is called "free trade." A better, more comprehensive expression for the same thing is the principle which is usually quoted incorrectly: *Laissez aller, laisser passer!* This principle condemns every type of economic barrier. Let things move out and come in freely. Let every commodity, every man, every kind of money move unmolested out of every country and into every country.

Well, at present it is considered fashionable to smile at the principle of *laissez passer*. It is simply not modern. What is considered modern is the principle followed in these matters by Louis XIV, Louis XV, Louis XVI, and George I, George II, and George III. True, these inspirers of our contemporary economic practices did not go so far in the art of obstruction as we have gone with our customs, contingents, import licenses, export licenses, transfer licenses, passports, visas, immigration quotas, residence permits, work permits, and so on. Nevertheless they were determined opponents of anarchic liberal world trade, which set in after their era in the nineteenth century. They were convinced that in all these matters the state must have a hand and defend higher interests. Unfortunately this condition more or less obtains again to-day. Those who utter the appeal "*laissez passer*" are answered only by a shrug of the shoulders. None the less, this appeal will not be silenced, for it will never cease to be true that the abandonment of the principle of *laissez passer* has been one of the most ominous self-mutilations of the capitalist system.

There is no doubt that the free international movement of commodities, people and capital is one of the most important elements of capitalism. Every student learns this during the first term of his course in economics. A system in which economic activity is not ordered from above, but in which hundreds of thousands of individual capitalists freely and separately do what they please requires mechanisms which "automatically" co-ordinate and regulate all this activity.

Now, one of the most important of these regulating "automatisms" is the free international movement of goods. When there is a shortage of one commodity in one country and its price rises, this commodity immediately flows in from another country and the shortage and rising price are stopped. Inversely, when a surplus with an attending drop in prices occurs anywhere, the cheaper goods are immediately bought up by traders from other countries, and the anomaly of excess disappears. The same is true of people and of capital. International free exchange creates the "currents" which continuously tend to level out shortages and over-production all over the world ; to make supply meet demand and demand meet supply; to transfer labour power and capital from places where they lie fallow to places where they can be used. And these currents alternate uninterruptedly; sometimes from week to week, sometimes from day to day. The flexibility with which they react to every displacement, however slight, is their essential meaning, like that of the balancing pole in the hands of the tightrope walker. This flexibility cannot be achieved or replaced by customs, regulations and quota laws, which are formulated slowly and remain rigid for years. On the contrary, such regulations and laws obstruct the channels of these currents, prevent them from flowing, rising, and falling. They cripple the "automatism." Bottlenecks, price crises, declines in production and sales, all the anomalies which are ironed out by this automatism, are no longer or only inadequately ironed out. The pulsations of economic life in the whole world and in each country separately become more erratic and irregular. Any slight indisposition anywhere becomes a grave, stubborn disease. The whole mechanism runs less efficiently, less productively.

Every student learns this, and it is not just theory. We had the system of international free trade once; we saw what it accomplished. It is a fact that England abolished her most important customs duties in 1846 and what remained of them in 1860, and that from then on, until long after the first World War, she was free and open for every foreign commodity. It is a fact that the British example was followed everywhere, although not always completely. It is a fact that until 1914 one could travel all over the

world without a passport or a visa except in the Czarist Empire.
It is a fact that everyone could settle anywhere. It is a fact that
the 105,000,000 people who inhabited the United States at the
time of the enactment of the immigration laws were composed
of two significantly unequal parts; only fifteen per cent were
descendants of those who had been in the country in 1800,
while 85 per cent were the immigrants of the century of freedom
and their descendants. It is a fact that capital could travel at
will and that the greater part of the industrial giant which grew
up in the United States during the last century was built with
foreign capital. Finally, it is a fact that under this system mankind
experienced by far the greatest economic upswing and social
progress in all its history. The record of the nineteenth century is
there for all to read.

How this fruitful system was destroyed no sooner than it
was established is a particularly tragic chapter in the history of
human folly. For it was destroyed largely without deliberate in-
tent. Here and there some powerful special interests succeeded in
reintroducing customs duties on their own behalf. (Particularly
characteristic and portentous was the reintroduction by Germany
of customs duties on two basic war raw materials, iron and grains,
in 1879.) But every economic branch that succeeded in doing this
nevertheless ardently desired the maintenance of free trade in
every other branch. But, as is usually the case, every step after
a certain period of time was followed by another, and after one
country applied one kind of restrictive measures, other countries
applied other kinds.

Almost all of them knew that they were producing poison.
Only a few cranks and provincials and isolationists were blind
enough to expect genuine advantage for their own country from
the growing barriers between the nations. During the period
between the two world wars, which saw the destruction of free
trade at an ever more rapid rate, characteristically enough not
a year went by without the governments which carried on the
process breaking out in bitter collective complaints about it.
Year after year they addressed warning speeches to one another
at conferences or League committees; they adjured one another
in unanimous resolutions to halt the march to disaster and even
to turn back on the path. But they neither halted nor turned
back. In 1931, when even England, the lonely last defender of
the faith, capitulated and began to build walls around herself

and when, simultaneously, Germany began to run amuck with the outbreak of her "autarchy" fever, one of the most vital organs of the capitalist system was definitely smashed.

When a country becomes socialistic it thereby ends all free trade by definition. Then the government fully controls all international exchanges. In its capacity as sole buyer, seller, and owner it alone produces all the international exchanges. Whatever one may think of this state of affairs, it is at least consistent. The amphibious condition to which the capitalist system was brought by its traitors is inconsistent. The tightrope walker whose balancing-pole has been made motionless is unable to exercise his art. The capitalist system with obstructed international currents was unable to function effectively. And the moment is approaching when mankind will once again face the question: What shall we do about this? No one, I should like to believe, would recommend a return to the conditions of 1939. No one will dare assert that capitalist economy can function in a world which is divided into sixty more or less watertight separate compartments. If these walls must be breached, why not tear them down completely? Why not return to real free trade?

The opportunity for this will be more favourable after the war than it was before and than it will be for a long time if it is missed then. Economically, the post-war world will find itself provisionally in a kind of vacuum. Normal peacetime international trade has stopped at present; in any case, it will have to develop anew, in quite different channels. The same is true of industrial production. Thus the phantom which in ordinary times barred the return to *laissez passer* will no longer exist. The breakdown of the frontiers under ordinary conditions meant the disturbance of the price level in all countries, a change in the direction of imports and exports, the destruction of many branches of industry and trade, and the creation of great difficulties in certain others. A violent and perhaps lengthy transitional crisis threatened. But after this war the situation will be very different. Everything will be dislocated in any case. Everything must be rearranged. This is a unique opportunity. There was no way out of an aberration which put economic life into a rigid strait jacket. There will be no way out of it if this strait jacket is put on again. But during a short period after the war, while the vacuum still prevails, we shall be free to choose our course. The course which fits the nature of the system is clear: total *laissez passer* among

countries that have a capitalist system, and total state trade
with a country like Russia, which itself totally controls its foreign
trade.

Strong prejudices which have long been nurtured will have
to be overcome. The pretexts under which the tariff walls were
erected in different countries were farcically contradictory. One
country represented them as a protection against the too cheap
products of more advanced countries; another as a protection
against the too cheap products of backward countries. Nevertheless, in every country there was a widespread belief in whatever pretext was fashionable. Yes, there is a certain belief in the
ideal of ships embarking fully laden and returning empty. There
is in the United States a certain belief in the advantage of wages
artificially pushed higher than abroad—as though prices, too,
were not also artificially pushed higher than abroad. There is a
certain belief in the theory that foreign trade can be neglected,
because it constitutes no more than eight to ten per cent. of the
national volume of business—as though, from the point of view
of unemployment, this ten per cent more or less were not of the
most tremendous importance. There is a certain belief in the
theory that immigration increases unemployment—as though,
aside from many other things, every immigrant did not, in addition to his labour power, bring his demands as a consumer. But
despite all the ballast of false teachings and prejudices, the single
demonstrated and irrefutable truth again and again emerges
that the capitalist system grew great through the free, not the
manipulated movement of commodities, people, and capital.
And the moment approaches when it will be decided, possibly
for a century, whether the capitalist system will find its way
back to earth.

There is no substitute for it. From everywhere comes the call
to get international trade into full swing again. But it strikes
one almost as a tragedy that to achieve this aim the most complicated government mechanisms are being recommended. To
be sure, several international mechanisms have always been
useful and will be so again. For instance, there have always been
international agreements concerning the protection of currencies
or international credits for weak countries. After the war such
things will be more necessary than ever. But to equip the shoe-
maker with proper tools is one thing, and to meddle in
his shoeshop is another. All the projects for furthering and

channelizing trade itself—that is, international buying and selling
—through cleverly conceived intergovernmental organizations
will in practice only constitute new fetters, inhibitions, and
obstructions to the capitalist mechanism. What, for instance,
is the purpose of securing "free access to the raw materials of
the world" through God knows what ingenious international
organs, pools, quotas, and condominiums? Was there ever the
slightest restriction on the free access to raw materials? Could
not every country and every firm in every country always buy
everything they wanted to buy; and could not some of them—
for instance, Germany and Japan, to our grief—do this only too
well? All these artificialities are not only superfluous in the
capitalist system; they are contrary to it. Let its future be what
its past was. That is the only way to give full play to its best
features.

We have here a second set of means of driving away the
Furies of the thirties. After the first over-all condition has been
fulfilled, after peace has been stabilized and the causes of extra-
economic devastations removed, profits and *laissez passer* are
the next remedies to be applied. They will enable the capitalist
system to function spontaneously better than in the era of its
mutilation. Thanks to them, depressions and unemployment
periods can be expected to remain within more normal limits.
I will clarify my point by quoting a figure which is meant only
as an illustration, not as a prophecy: the future attacks of unemployment will be half as severe and half as long as the ones we
experienced in the thirties.

And this is not all. There are still third-line remedies. These
are the palliatives. The less severe unemployment crises, which
will occur, can be considerably further weakened by emergency
measures.

One of these measures is a more systematic policy of spreading the work—and here an analogy with an old and hallowed
capitalist institution comes to mind. I am referring to the official
rate of discount which is raised or lowered by the central bank
of each country in accordance with the transformations of the
business cycle and the plethora or shortage of money on the
market. By simple fiat it increases or decreases the cost of borrowed
money all over the country, with telling effects. It would be
logical to treat labour time as a fluid element, too, and, in
accordance with the business cycle, to increase or decrease its

length by an official "rate." If we designate normal working time by 100 per cent., in times of sinking prosperity it could be reduced by simple fiat all over the country to 90, 80, or 70 per cent. The existing jobs would be better distributed among the workers than by the erratic methods hitherto applied. Although some minor difficulties will have to be solved, the principle is to be recommended.

Much more important is a second palliative: that of public spending. To the extent that the capitalists' investments decrease, the government should multiply its orders and purchases. Volumes have been written on this subject, and the discussion cannot be reproduced here. The main thing is that this intervention of the public authorities should not materialize only in a few gigantic works projects at a few scattered points, but that it spread all over the country. Every public administration, from the smallest municipality up to the central government, should work out mobilization plans for the depression during every period of prosperity. The plan must be in the files ready to be put into operation. It is still falsely believed that such a policy is harmful to the capitalist system. Not at all! While this system excludes the state as a producer or trader, it has always welcomed the state as a consumer and customer. There is also some grumbling to the effect that such a policy is impossible without increasing the public debt. But people will have to get used to the idea that in national emergencies the public debt must inevitably grow. In our world there is no getting away from the fact that the government—in contrast to the private citizen—can save in good times, but must increase expenditures in bad times. And the fear of this is unjustified. To put it in American terms, two billion dollars could finance an amount of works and purchases that would directly and indirectly give work to one million workers for the period of one year. Thus the cost of one year of world war could give employment to almost two million workers during all the depressions of a whole century. There is no doubt that it is possible to go very far in the direction of government-made work without causing any serious damage.

The palliatives are the third line of defence. Let me again express my point in figures and say that depressions already reduced to half their former severity can be halved again by the third-line expedients.

Even then there will be a certain number of cyclic unemployed from time to time. Here we come to the fourth line of defence. Society can and should take care of those who are struck by unemployment.

That society has this duty cannot be quibbled away. Those who prefer the liberal economic system, despite the fact that now and again it inevitably makes a certain number of people breadless, must be ready to make up for this deficiency of their preferred system. Provisions for the maintenance of the unemployed during the temporary depressions must be made—and the possibilities here go very far. Even those who had no job have always lived; they have eaten and have been sheltered, however badly. This alone proves that the pot of social wealth is full enough to afford a portion for them, too. At present, developments are impending which will give the care of the jobless a character entirely different from what it has been hitherto. Unemployment relief no longer must or can have the character of a favour. If temporary unemployment is a normal occurrence, a mechanism which insures the existence of its temporary victims is normal, too. It is now recognized that social insurance provides such a mechanism.

There is nothing new or revolutionary in the system of social insurance. As a nation-wide obligatory institution it was introduced for the first time by an arch-conservative in a conservative country. It was Bismarck who between 1880 and 1890 created insurance against illness, accidents, disability, and old age for the German workers and employees. This policy of "sound socialism," as he called it, was opposed by both the Right and the Left. To the latter it was not socialist enough; to the former, not sound enough. But Bismarck's example was imitated. From Germany the idea of social insurance spread over Europe and later to the other continents. The types of insurance gradually grew more varied, the circle of the insured grew gradually wider, and the premiums gradually higher. But it was several decades before people began to think of unemployment, too, as an evil against which one could be insured. And the first steps toward full unemployment insurance made between the two world wars were hesitating. Even the British Beveridge Plan, which has justly aroused so much attention throughout the world, on this score shows traces of that caution with which one moves over unexplored terrain. It is an admirable plan. Although it refers only to England and is designed for English conditions alone, it seems destined to prove an important stage in the international development of social insurance. It is not too fantastic to conceive its historical importance as a kind of counterpart to the Magna Charta. The doctrine that the individual can and must be insured against every conceivable economic emergency "from the cradle to the grave" will triumphantly sweep the world. Nevertheless, it may be doubted that this plan goes as far as it might in its provisions for the unemployed.

The difficulties inherent in any scheme of unemployment insurance are obvious. So long as man is what he is, there must be a difference between the incomes of those who are working and those who are not. If idleness were as profitable as work, the temptation not to do anything at all would be too great. Therefore the insurance premium must be kept lower than the normal wage. But how much lower? Must it be lower by fifty per cent or will thirty per cent be sufficient? Only experience can enlighten us on this point. But I should like to believe that even an income which is only thirty per cent lower than the norm will generally be felt sufficiently inadequate to keep the urge to work again alive. The standard rate provided for in the Beveridge Plan (forty shillings a week) is lower.

It would be misleading to translate the British rates into dollars: the price levels in the two countries are too different. Other British peculiarities, not typical of other countries, may also play a part. In the 350 to 520 million pounds sterling which the total "cradle to the grave" plan demands as an annual contribution from the state treasury, unemployment is represented by the relatively small item of 110 million pounds. The reasons which make this sum appear as a maximum in the eyes of the British Exchequer are not necessarily valid in other countries. This figure is based on the assumption that, on the average, eight and one half per cent. of adults of both sexes will always be jobless. If all the other means and palliatives are applied, this figure seems excessive. Generally speaking, with a view to the situation in the world as a whole and not in Great Britain alone, it can be said that the premiums for the unemployed can certainly be made higher, and even if this does not take place immediately, it will take place a few years later.

More particularly, voluntary private supplementary insurance will be possible; and this point is of especial interest for the middle classes, which the Beveridge Plan, that international model, draws for the first time into the group of insured persons. It is entirely right in doing so. The idea that only workers and employees suffer from depressions was discredited long ago. No less and often more hit by depressions are the small business men whose shops are ruined and the professionals who lose their clients—and for them it is often much harder than for the worker to rise again in a new period of prosperity. No scheme of unemployment insurance can leave these groups out in the future. And if they are enabled to insure themselves against ruin by the negative business cycles beyond the official rates, the general situation will be improved further. This problem seems solvable.

However that may be, if after sixty years of existence social insurance makes the strides we may expect it to make after the war, something extraordinary will be achieved. An element will be introduced into the fabric of the capitalist system which has hitherto been absent from it: security. If provisions are made against all situations of distress, including unemployment and insolvency, to such a point that no individual can any longer fall into abject misery, the whole character of the struggle for existence will change. Man will no longer struggle for bread. He will hardly struggle for the butter on his bread. He will struggle for the ham and the sardines on his buttered bread. Bare subsistence will be secured. Man's efforts and preoccupations will be directed toward what exceeds bare subsistence.

This means a material and psychological transformation of incalculable scope. It frees us of panic with regard to future depressions and periods of unemployment. If through peace, profits, and *laissez passer* we can reduce by half the intensity of the depressions and if through palliatives we can again halve this half, we no longer need tremble before the problems still left. Individually and collectively we can look upon them as department stores look upon the fact that a certain percentage of their goods disappears without a trace. This fact is taken into account in the general budget. To be sure, during every seven- or ten-year cycle a country like the United States will have, let us say, three million unemployed for a period of two or three years; but this will be provided in the national budget. To be sure, within the decades every man will be exposed to the hazard of being without a job for a year or two; but this will be taken into account in every individual's expectations. If the subsistence of all those affected is secured, the whole phenomenon of unemployment will become different in character. From the collective point of view it will still remain unpleasant, but it will no longer be a terror, a scourge, a plague, and a disgrace. From an individual point of view it will still not be a welcome holiday episode, but it will cease to be materially and morally a tragedy and martyrdom. The horrible symbol of war veterans peddling apples in the streets will be seen no longer.

We can agree that *the depressions of the capitalist system can be freed of their terrors. Their severity and length can be drastically reduced, and their victims can be protected against want.*

CHAPTER TWENTY-FIVE

THE WORKING MAN UNDER SOCIALISM

THE CAPITALIST SYSTEM can emasculate the dragon of unemployment and create secure shelters against his attacks. The socialist system can do more: it can slay the dragon.

There is no argument on this question. The facts are conclusive. There is no unemployment in Soviet Russia. Nor was there any in Nazi Germany. The two regimes have used this absence of unemployment, which stood out so dramatically against the background of the world crisis, as the chief argument in their propaganda—and in propaganda this superiority in one respect naturally became superiority in all respects. But the propagandist additions, adornments, and exaggerations did not discredit the truth itself. The truth is that a railroad is something different from a hundred thousand private cars. If economic activity springs from hundreds of thousands of completely unconnected sources of will, there must occasionally be disturbances and as a result of these a certain number of idle hands. If all economic activity springs from one source, from the will of one single authority, which alone and unchecked rules over all tools and resources, there is no reason why this authority should ever permit any hands to be idle. There is nothing obscure or controversial about this. If our main objective is the radical and absolute elimination of unemployment, socialism must be adopted.

But the question is what other effects this will produce. And to begin with let us consider the other economic effects; for the time being, we shall disregard the non-economic effects, which are more important.

Let us assume that the great socialist transformation has taken place. The means of production have been expropriated, and they are in the hands of the state. Those who tried to prevent this have been overcome, gently or ungently. The sceptics are silenced. The faithful have had their triumph and celebrated the realization of their great dream. Now ten years have passed. Everyday life has come again. There is no unemployment—this is an established fact. Even the word has disappeared from the language. A machine, a motor, a counter, a desk await all the people all the time. Very well, then, what else? Which of the other immense hopes—the economic ones—will have been realized in these ten years?

Quite certainly we can no longer expect that the hope of equality will be realized. Those who expected it will be disappointed. Just as before, there will be high, medium, and low incomes, and the same old pyramid of different standards of living. Naturally, the high incomes will no longer be received by the same persons as before; instead of Mr. Smith it will be Mr. Jones. Even more naturally, the high incomes will come from a different source: instead of being salaries and dividends paid by private enterprises, they will be salaries and remunerations granted by the state. But this will not change anything for the millions, who now, as before, will have low incomes. The pyramid will still exist. They will be at its bottom, and somebody else will be at the top.

No illusions about this are possible any longer. The old controversy as to whether all incomes and living standards can be levelled must to-day be regarded as settled. It must be noted that the controversy was never concerned with the technical possibility of execution: with the help of the necessary laws and agencies incomes could be levelled. What was disputed was always only whether the motor of economic activity could run efficiently under such conditions. Around 1850 or 1900 the two opposing parties could not prove anything in this controversy. "It won't work!" said the sceptics. "The old Adam will not function without the incentive of individual advantages." "It will work!" said the enthusiasts. "The old Adam will change." One prediction was as good as another. But then the experiment was made. The Bolsheviks of the first years tried desperately to run their machine under the regime of equality. It did not work. As early as 1921 Lenin himself felt compelled to reintroduce unequal incomes to a large extent along with his famous "New Economic Policy." Up to the present day, this has been not only continued but intensified under changing forms. The differences in remuneration have grown greater and greater. A factory manager soon received an income a hundred or a hundred and fifty times as great as that of his workers, not counting his many other advantages. Official Russian sources reported with praise how individual patriots had subscribed more than a million roubles in war bonds—and these millions must have been earned, and earned during the last few years. The reason for all this was not a perverse whim of Stalin's, but bare necessity. The prediction of the sceptics of 1900, not that of the optimists, proved correct. The old Adam showed himself incorrigible. Under the system of equal incomes economic life simply bogged down. There was no way of getting anything out of the people beyond that minimum which can be enforced by control and supervision. To achieve the necessary higher efficiency, inequality in incomes had to be re-established. Thus the test was made and it was shown that even a socialist system cannot function unless it inflames the energies, will, and interest of the people by the old, unjust, but irreplaceable incentive of inequality. Ten years after the establishment of socialism the common man will be, just as he was before, part of an economic hierarchy. In this respect socialism will not bring him any particular satisfaction.

Very well then, if the hoped-for equality will beyond all doubt remain unrealized, the second question arises: How will the economic situation of the common man be changed? Putting aside all comparisons with the higher income group, how much income, well-being, and abundance will the lower strata have after ten years of socialism?

One thing need no longer be discussed very much: the popular idea of socialism—that is, "sharing." The naïve imagine that the fantastic incomes of the du Ponts and Rockefellers will be taken away from them and divided among all the people; as a result the people will fare much better. Now, this was never scientific socialism. The simplest arithmetical calculation refutes this idea. Take all American incomes after deduction of taxes and throw them into one pot. Divide the contents of the pot uniformly among the entire population. The result will be that the lowest earners will have a whole three hundred dollars a year more than before—which certainly does not constitute abundance—while even incomes of as little as two thousand dollars a year will be cut. Hence, scientific socialism never expected a great improvement in the lot of the little man merely from the levelling of incomes. But we have found that such a levelling will never take place at all. So all discussion of this subject is superfluous.

Socialism expects abundance for the common man from a quite different source. If we reduce the matter to essentials, we can say that socialism expects abundance from a gigantic increase and expansion of production. And socialism results in such an expansion of production; only socialism can bring it and will bring it without fail. As Lenin put it in *State and Revolution*: "The expropriation of the means of production will make a gigantic development of the productive forces possible. And seeing how incredibly, even now, capitalism retards this development, how much progress could be made on the basis of modern technique even at the level it has reached, we have a right to say, with the fullest confidence, that the expropriation of the capitalists will inevitably result in a gigantic development of the productive forces of human society." Thus a great rise in the common man's well-being is expected from a grandiose economic advance such as is impossible under capitalism.

Very well, then, how much of this unprecedented development of the productive forces will materialize after ten years of socialism?

Once again we enter upon the field of an old controversy—the decisive one in so far as economic issues are involved. Will the development of productivity be greater under socialism than under capitalism? On this point, too, in 1850, 1900, or even in 1920 the predictions of the opposing parties were contradictory and impossible of proof. The Socialists and their opponents had their favourite arguments. The Socialists said: "Under our system the wheels will turn constantly, without slowing up as a result of crises and depressions; there will be no waste of capital or labour, such as is now created by competitive struggles and lack of planning." These were weighty arguments. But their opponents replied that these socialist advantages would be cancelled out by a number of drawbacks. They maintained that the State as sole entrepreneur would accomplish less than the multiplicity of capitalist entrepreneurs. If your economic machine does always work at full speed, they said, it will work much more clumsily, more expensively, and less productively than capitalism, because it will be managed by an entrepreneur who is never threatened by competition or bankruptcy. And they added: if you do not suffer from the defects of planlessness, every error in your plans will have repercussions a hundred times greater than those committed under our system; moreover, a thousand times more possibilities will remain unexploited. These arguments were no less weighty. In the absence of any kind of practical test, no one could say which of these two predictions would prove correct.

But now the experiment has been made. We have twenty-five years of socialist economy in Russia to go by. Of these the first years may not count, because they were years of confusion and transition. And we have no data about the last years, for by 1938 the Soviet government had ceased publishing figures. But concerning the ten years between 1928 and 1938 there are enough official Russian statistics to give us a picture of the economic progress made under socialism in an interpretation which is doubtless favourable. And these were ten years of a particularly rapid advance, the years in which the first two Five-Year Plans were carried out.

It goes without saying that during these ten years Russian economy expanded greatly. A mighty development of the productive forces was accomplished. But this is not the question here; the question is, whether the rate and the tempo of this growth were greater than they could have been under capitalism, thus demonstrating the superiority of the socialist system. And the sober truth is that the rate of growth during the ten heroic years of Russia was considerably slower than the rate of growth attained in capitalist countries at similar stages of development. Let us compare these rates.

To begin with, let us dispel an error that has assumed grotesque proportions. Under the influence of intensive propaganda the idea has taken root that the socialist system in Russia had to begin from scratch, as it were. It is believed that the Soviet found a purely agrarian Middle Ages in Russia, and that their first task was to wrench the beginnings of a modern economy from desert ground. Therefore Russia is allegedly a case that cannot be compared with any other. This is a thesis which does not correspond in the slightest degree to the actual facts, and it is refuted by witnesses whom even Communists must recognize.

These witnesses are Marx, Engels, and Lenin. As early as 1882 Marx and Engels, in a preface for a Russian edition of the *Communist Manifesto*, wrote about "the feverish development of capitalism in Russia." As far back as 1899 Lenin devoted a whole book to *The Development of Capitalism in Russia*. In it he stated that Russian economy had entered upon "a period of feverish upswing." He spoke of the "technical revolution which at present is taking place in Russia." He noted in various branches "a development which proceeds more rapidly than in western Europe, partly even than in North America." He described the "immense expansion of big industrial centres and the appearance of a number of new centres." "The number of Russian factories is rapidly increasing." "The rapid development of industry in Russia is creating an immense and ever growing market for means of production, but the market for objects of individual consumption is also increasing rapidly."

As I have said, this was written as far back as 1899. In the following years the development was even more rapid. Between 1890 and 1913 the annual Russian production of iron increased nine-fold. Extraction of coal rose more than five times. During one single year —the last year of capitalist peace, 1913—Russia's total industrial output rose by no less than twenty per cent—and, incidentally, her production of wheat did not cease to remain the biggest in the world. In brief, Russia's industrialization began a few decades later than that of other capitalist states, but then it galloped forward at terrific speed. An official Soviet *Outline of the History of the October Revolution*, published during Lenin's lifetime, correctly described the situation in the following words: "Russia was rapidly moving along the capitalist lines of development, overtaking the older capitalist countries which had gone ahead."

Very few people know these facts; actually they have gradually been veiled. But they suffice to raise the question whether socialization has brought Russia farther than she would have come merely by continuing her own capitalist development at the same rate she had already achieved. It is impossible to prove what would have been, if . . . . There is no way of ascertaining irrefutably how Russia would have developed if socialism had not been adopted there. But we can ascertain how other, non-socialist countries in a comparable economic stage did develop. Let us, for instance, compare a few Russian rates of growth with their equivalents in the United States.

Let us begin with coal. In 1928, at the beginning of the heroic decade of the Five-Year Plans, Russia produced 34·9 million long tons of coal. In 1938 the output had risen to 130·8 million— an impressive leap! Now let us take America. A comparable point of departure here is the year 1870. The United States then produced 29 million long tons a year. Ten years later the output rose to 63·1 million. The leap seems less impressive, but this is precisely one of those optical illusions which confused so many minds. In fact the American leap is much more impressive. One must take into account the fact that the average Russian population at the period in question was 160 million, while that of the United States was only 44 million. More people can produce more—and need more. Thus one is compelled to divide the absolute increase by the population; then we obtain something which might be called the index of growth. Now, with regard to coal production, the indices of growth of both countries in two equivalent decades are 599 for Russia and 795 for the United States. Actually, the capitalist rate of growth was far higher than the socialist one. And this is not all. The socialist rate of growth was achieved with modern technical devices—for instance, electric drills. The considerably higher capitalist rate of growth was achieved with the old-fashioned tools of the 1870's: without electricity, with picks and shovels. In later decades, with modern machines, the American indices of growth are even more impressive. In the decade from 1890 to 1900 the American coal industry achieved an index of growth of 1332—more than double what was achieved during the heroic decade in Russia.

I have applied this method of comparison to branch after branch, and the picture is almost uniformly the same everywhere. Establish the point of departure in any important branch from which Russia started in 1928. Go back to the year in which the same point was achieved in America. Then find the increase of production in the two countries during the ten subsequent years and divide these rates by the respective populations. All along the line you will discover that the socialist growth is smaller than the capitalist growth during the corresponding decades. For iron, for instance, the indices are 70 for Russia, 96 for the United States. For oil they are 725 and 1735; for copper, 410 and 1598. The discrepancies are even greater in the manufacturing industry. The expansion of railroad construction in Russia during the heroic decade is measured by an index of 38; during the equivalent American decade—sixty years earlier—by an index of 918. In the production of motor vehicles of all kinds the Russian index is 129; the American for the equivalent decade is 2060. And although exactly the same method of comparison cannot be applied to agricultural production because the picture is disturbed by the accident of good and bad harvests, it is worth noting that in this respect also—and here more than elsewhere —the socialist rate of growth is considerably lower than the capitalist one.

This method must be applied if the rate of the socialist "development of the productive forces" is to be compared with the rate of the capitalist development. I know that even this method is not absolutely foolproof or absolutely comprehensive ; but we have no better one at our disposal, and it gives us not mere assertions, but the results of actual experimentation. It is objected that the experiment cannot be considered typical: "Only in Russia was it so; with us it will be different." Much stress, for instance, is laid upon the argument that in 1928 Russia consisted only of medieval peasants who had to be taught the rudiments of modern labour methods. But we have already touched upon this subject. There was in Russia a considerable group of skilled industrial workers. And, on the other hand, the immigrants who in the 1870's and 1880's streamed into the mines and steel mills of Pennsylvania were for the most part raw human material. Foreigners who worked in Russia between 1928 and 1938 have published detailed accounts of their experiences. From them it is clear enough that the decisive drawbacks did not stem from specifically Russian qualities, but from the general nature of the state as entrepreneur. The phenomena we know in the field of administration in every state were reproduced in the much more sensitive economic field. The fact that this entrepreneur did not have to fear competition or bankruptcy had its effects. Every undertaking required considerably more personnel and time than under the system of private enterprise. Every question had to travel from agency to agency and became the object of long and arduous investigations and deliberations. Conflict of competence and opinion between the various departments had a continually parlayzing effect. There was a

generalized fear of deviating from the routine; there was the
natural aversion of every highly centralized machinery to diversity
and allegedly superfluous new activities. And one single miscal-
culation at the top produced cumulative consequences down to
the last cog.

Taken in their sum, these drawbacks of the socialist process
were more significant than its assets. The investments and production that were undertaken devoured much more labour and
material—they were "more expensive"—than under the capitalist system; and as a result a great number of investments and
productions that would have been undertaken under capitalism
were omitted. Amid superhuman efforts immense progress was
doubtless made. But because of the nature of the entrepreneur—
the state—the rate of advance was in the end smaller than that
demonstrated by the capitalist system at the price of far lesser
efforts. And it is needless to add that nothing is changed in these
lessons by the impressive showing of the Russian war. Russia's
military triumphs reflect many things—among others, the
economic fact that her productive capacity has grown. But her
glorious victories do not throw any new light on the specific,
strictly limited question whether this capacity has grown at a
rate faster than the capitalist one.

Now, then, this is the test of which we clearly see the results
before us. One prediction is no longer as good as another.
Practical experience has confirmed the sceptical prediction.
The immense hopes founded in socialism have no prospect of
realization. Ten years after the introduction of socialism the
productive forces would probably be further expanded. But one
must stubbornly ignore the demonstrated facts to hope to-day
that they would be expanded more than if the old system had
been preserved.

In consequence, the same would be true of the higher standards
of living after ten years of socialism—those higher standards of
living which are expected to result from the gigantic development of the productive forces. Economic matters would be discussed infinitely more than they are to-day. A number of items
which previously were noted at most on the business pages of
the newspapers would fill the front pages. Every factory opened
anywhere would be cited as a proof of the vitality of the new
system. The draining of every swamp would be celebrated as
an amazing achievement. And probably, although by no means

certainly, the general standard of living would have risen after ten years. But there is no real indication that it would have risen more—let alone infinitely more—than it would have risen under the old system. The real indication is that it would have risen less.

It might be retorted that the rise of living standards is not so important as all that. The protagonists of "basic changes" might say: "Even if no great material advances are achieved, so what?" In fact, this point of view can be defended. It is not a socialist point of view, but it is a point of view. When a condition has been reached in which man has what we might call the necessities, all further material progress is of very controversial philosophic value. It certainly does not produce more happiness. We are not happier than our parents were without electric lights, telephones, nylon stockings, refrigerators, radios, movies, automobiles, and trolley cars. People become unhappy when they must do without things to which they have been accustomed or when they must do without things considered normal in their environment. They do not become unhappy because no new things are added to their store of comforts. If the socialist declared: "We are not particularly interested in economic progress; what we want is mainly a condition of equality and security, and it is a matter of minor importance for us whether there will be a movement upwards from there"—if they declared this, they would have less popular appeal, but their position would have a certain philosophic distinction. They would come closer to their predecessors, the communists of the Christian era. However, they declare the opposite of this. They declare that their aim is a greater rise in living standards than has ever been achieved before. And they maintain that in this very respect their system will prove superior to capitalism. The facts are evidence against this thesis. It is hope, dream, vision, fiction. It is not real.

Emotion, which in such matters blocks calm thinking, will prevent many from agreeing with us. It is none the less true that *the living standards of the common man are likely to rise more slowly, not more rapidly, under socialism than under capitalism.*

CHAPTER TWENTY-SIX

WHAT PRICE FREEDOM?

BUT ALL THIS is unimportant! Socialism makes its principal appeal on economic grounds, but, paradoxical as this may sound, its economic aspects are in the last analysis secondary. It raises a problem of a quite different nature, a problem which towers above the economic one as the Himalayas tower above the cliffs of Dover. This problem is to what extent socialism imperils human freedom. And what we are discussing here is not the freedom of millionaires. No, it is your, our, my freedom that is in question. Nor is it the perverted thing represented as "freedom" by modern sophists that concerns us, but freedom without sophisms, the one for which testimony has been given in prison and exile, on gallows and battlefields, in every period of history.

Frankly, if this were not the problem, it would hardly be worth while to argue, it certainly would not be worth while to fight about it. The prospect that socialism will slow up rather than hasten economic progress would not suffice to excite men's minds. They would be disappointed in their expectations; but, after all, they are used to that. If their faith and will are so strong, let them put their socialism into practice. Mankind will manage to get along with less economic progress. In fact, since they will be compensated for this by the abolition of unemployment, they will manage all the better. A lowered rate of economic upswing alone would not be worth any counter-agitation, determined resistance, tragedy.

But even if the economic aspects of socialism were as wonderful as its proponents say and believe, this alone would not justify any ecstatic enthusiasm for it. It would still have to be ascertained what price must be paid for the economic gains in terms of freedom; it would still have to be decided—and in full knowledge of the dilemma, not in ignorance or frivolity—whether the will to pay this price really exists. The economic discussion skims only the surface of the problem of "basic changes." At bottom, it is immaterial who is right or wrong in this discussion. The serious fundamental—I would even say the tragic—core of this problem remains unaffected by it. That core is the question of freedom.

Let us avoid all abstractions. Socialism means that there will be only one employer in the country. The advancement, success, indeed the daily bread of every single man would be in the hands of that single employer. He alone could give jobs. He alone would decide whether you go up or remain down below. From him alone you would receive your bread, not to mention the butter on it. From him there would be no escape. You could no longer slam the door in the face of this employer, who would no longer be one in a hundred thousand, but the only one. You could not look for another, for there would be no other. You could not escape into an independent way of making your living, for this would not exist, either. The prayer: "Give us this day our daily bread," would, in point of fact, become a prayer addressed to the monopolistic employer, the state.

It is not at all necessary to assume that this monopolistic employer would be a hard boss, although this, too, is possible. We can readily suppose that in the factories and shops and offices and laboratories everything would be irreproachable and that the content of the pay envolepes would be generous. This has nothing to do with the great problem. The great problem is that the state would be irresistible.

Who would be able to risk its displeasure? The laws might say a hundred times that you had the right to your own opinion, but they would no longer be a guarantee. They would protect you—as far as they went!—from arbitrary actions of the police, the courts, and the prisons. But they would not protect you from not obtaining the better position to which you aspired nor from losing the one you had. And this single fact would be more powerful than all the rights and freedoms. Against a government that controlled everyone's subsistence no one could really take advantage of his rights and freedoms. To arouse the displeasure of such a government would be suicidal. If it asked anything of you, you could no longer refuse; you would risk being turned into the street a month later, under some pretext or other. Even more impossible than to resist individually would be any kind of general organized opposition. No one could risk being a candidate against a government candidate, if this were connected with the danger of economic excommunication. No one could lead opposition parties or belong to them, start or support campaigns, call meetings and speak at them, if these were contrary to the wishes of the government. Yes, even if through some supreme inconsistency the newspapers escaped becoming state property, they would still be unable to express any kind of opposition. The government, as owner of the printing plants and paper factories, would be able to create the most unbearable difficulties for them. The editors and writers who as a rule have ambitions to become playwrights, novelists, screen or radio writers and commentators, would not dare to expose themselves to the vengeance of the sole play-producer, publisher, moving-picture producer, and radio-station owner. When the government is everyone's only bread-giver, any opposition becomes a piece of foolhardiness which no normal person would risk. And there are always more people ready to suffer the death of a hero in battle than to rot in civilian life.

This is the real danger of socialism. A dreadful power is inherent in the means of subsistence. Alexander Hamilton, in the classical language of the *Federalist*, warned of this. "In the general course of human nature," he wrote, "a power over a man's subsistence amounts to a power over his will." But there are various degrees of power over a man's subsistence. The more easily a man can change the means of subsistence he has for another, the less power it has. General Motors Corporation has great power over a sub-manager who earns thirty thousand dollars a year and could find an equally lucrative job only with great difficulty. This sub-manager can be ordered around by General Motors—if it wishes to order him around—to a fairly considerable extent, even in regard to his private life. But in normal times General Motors has very little power over an ordinary worker, who can get approximately equal wages elsewhere if he does not like his job. And another important consideration must be added: there are also various degrees of interest that an employer can show in his employees' will. A normal employer is rather indifferent to what his employees think, do, or want in matters that are not connected with his business. The radius of his interests is not so large that he needs to exert power over the whole radius of their interests. But for the employer who is the *state*, not only matters concerning one business are important; countless other matters are important, too. Each man's will interests him in innumerable respects. He has a far greater incentive to take real advantage of his power over people's wills.

Should we not therefore tremble before the prospect of a social order in which there is only one single master over all the means of subsistence, and in which this single master is the state?

A witness who knew something about this has warned us. Lenin himself explained quite clearly the meaning of state power over the bread of every individual. This significant statement is in *Peasants and Workers*. He was referring not to the printed notes called money, which are the usual means of getting one's daily bread, but to the printed notes called ration-cards, which are a different way of getting one's daily bread. If these two kinds of printed notes can be handed to you only by the state, then both of them represent its monopolistic power over your daily bread; and this is what Lenin said about the meaning of full state power over the people's daily bread: "The ration books . . . are in the hands of the Proletarian State, the most powerful means of control. Those means will furnish a power unprecedented in the annals of history. Those means of control and compulsion are stronger than the laws of the convent and the guillotine."

"Unprecedented . . . stronger than the guillotine"! Why mince words when one wants to speak frankly? In the hands of the government that wants to use it, the power over everybody's subsistence amounts to a guillotine over everybody's free-will. Once in possession of this power, it can decapitate all the liberties of a country within a very short time. Let me repeat that in order to achieve this result it hardly needs to violate any laws, for no law can ever prescribe when an employer should find an employee satisfactory and when he can find him unsatisfactory. For this reason tyranny will be able to develop in spite of the barriers of the existing laws as easily as rats pass under a fence.

It is difficult for the human mind to imagine things which it has not seen. For the inhabitants of a free country it seems almost impossible clearly to understand the process through which freedom is lost. One must have personally witnessed it once in order to realize its nature. As a rule, those who have never witnessed it, always remain too innocent about it. They think of the conditions to which they are accustomed. "It can't happen here." Why should anything change much? The state will become the sole owner of everything, but for the rest—so people imagine—everything will remain as it is. The old institutions and mechanisms, the Constitution, the Bill of Rights, opposition, parties, elections, parliaments, courts, all this will continue to function the day after socialism just as it did the day before. What a

7

delusion! Everything can change. The single fact that every-body's bread is in the power of the government sterilizes all these institutions and mechanisms, even if they continue to exist in name. The right to speak against the state is of no value if no one dares exercise it. Mechanisms for the control of the State are of no value if the people, who are the life of these mechan-isms, are compelled to behave in a servile fashion. From the moment this monopolistic power falls into the hands of the state for the first time, the people who will then be entirely dependent upon it will become more and more cautious. The moment the guillotine of the withdrawal of subsistence falls on the necks of a few overbold dissidents, the sclerosis of the political organism will set in. The blood which is still flowing through its old veins will be poisoned by fear. The body will no longer move, but will be moved. And once things have gone thus far, there will be no obstacle to transforming at will even the nominally subsisting institutions and mechanisms, the constitutions, bills of rights, and laws. Freedom will be lost. The black-out will descend.

"But my government will not do this," replies the optimist. "It will be a government which I myself have chosen and put in power. It will be composed of people whom I know, who all their lives have fought for the cause of the people and for free-dom. I can entrust my welfare to them without fear." It can be said that behind all the enthusiasm for "basic economic changes" there is a confidence that the governments which will wield the increased power will be benevolent and noble and self-restrained. This is an assumption which the optimists, whether they know it or not, simply cannot do without. The leaders think: "I will be the government," and that settles the matter as far as they are concerned. The followers think: "This will be my government, and I can be sure that it will not abuse the instrument of increased power—at least it will not abuse it against me." But one has no right to be sure of any government—least of all, of the unknown government of to-morrow. We cannot put ourselves blindly into anyone's hands. "*Se méfier c'est l'essence de la liberté.*" ("Dis-trust is the essence of freedom"), says Montesquieu. Even what is in the minds of those who have fought all their lives for the cause of freedom is, in reality, never quite clear. When such people achieve power, they often enough show surprisingly different faces. And even aside from this, hardly any government has ever refrained from using the full measure of power it had.

When difficult situations and crises arise, when opposition threatens, every government goes to the extreme limit of its actual power. Yes, perhaps the more firmly they are convinced that they are right and beneficent, the more readily they go to this extreme limit. Good intentions are one of the most common bridges to tyranny; the road to hell is paved with good intentions.

Are any economic advantages worth this dreadful price? Even if the economic hopes of socialism came true, would this compensate us for the loss of freedom? Would it compensate even for the loss of part of our freedom? Would it compensate even for the establishment of a regime which implied a grave danger to freedom?

The genuine socialists of the Marxian school were at least clear in this respect. They declared roundly that what we call freedom did not interest them. What they proclaimed was explicitly dictatorship. They called it dictatorship of the proletariat —which is again an illusion, because a dictatorship can be exercised only by an individual or by a few individuals. Their minds were quite made up that a dictatorship was to rule. And Lenin explained: "The very meaning of the word 'dictatorship' signifies the existence of an absolute government which is not limited by any laws, takes no notice of any rules whatsoever, and relies directly on violence."

These socialists, too, believed that dictatorship would disappear some day. But it must be emphasized that they promised a curious, not very reassuring kind of disappearance. Dictatorship was to pass away only after a very long period of transition— "after a whole historical epoch has elapsed." And the process of its disappearance was to be accomplished by virtue of a mystic apotheosis that, with the best will in the world, does not sound very convincing. The end of the dictatorship, we are told, will not come because it will be abolished; no, something much more grandiose and mysterious will take place. After socialism has ruled for a whole epoch, the state will disappear. Such a perfect harmony will set in that no state or government will any longer be necessary. "The state withers away," as Marx put it. "The state renders itself superfluous . . . it dies," as Engels commented. Unfortunately they never told us in greater detail what the world would look like in this paradisiac condition, without states and governments. Although this millennium is the proclaimed final goal and ultimate justification of the whole socialist adventure, any concrete description of it has so far not been vouchsafed to us. To-day most socialists do not seem to know anything at all about this last goal of their journey. It is no longer mentioned—least of all in Moscow. The bulk of to-day's socialists thus have no idea of how distant and how extremely uncertain the end of the dictatorship is, according to their own doctrine; they do not realize that it would depend upon an absolutely unsubstantiated miracle. But be that as it may, the genuine Communists and Marxian socialists cannot be reproached with being obscure, deluded, or irresolute in the matter of freedom. The socialist doctrine is unequivocal on the point that freedom as we know it must actually be sacrificed, and sacrificed for an indefinite period.

But do you, reader, share this resolute contempt for freedom? If people were clearly confronted with this dilemma, would any proportion of them worth mentioning consent to abandon even a part of their freedom, were it only for the duration of a "historical epoch," until that fata-morgana world without states and governments was achieved? Despite all the confusions, the opposite is certain! Confronted with this dilemma clearly, understandably, without any hocus-pocus, the overwhelming majority in the democratic countries would refuse to sacrifice their traditional rights and freedoms for the sake of any other advantage. So let us make the dilemma clear instead of obscuring it by sophisms. Let us establish clearly that there is hardly a surer way to lose all freedom than to make the state the monopolistic owner, employer, and feeder. Tragic is the error of those who dream of being able to lead mankind upwards on this path. For it is the path downwards. Tragic is the role of those who hope to attain a flourishing liberalism by following this road. They would lead all liberalism into the desert.

Tragic, indeed, is the role of so many liberals in this matter. Nothing has changed in the ultimate philosophy of the liberal camp, which is my camp. Now, as before, the basic ideals of this camp are those of humanity: the rights, sovereignty, dignity, and inviolability of the individual. It has never been more necessary to fight for these ideals than it is to-day. Without groups and centres which constantly and tenaciously wage the struggle for these ideals, conditions would soon degenerate everywhere. To-day the liberal mission is more imporant than ever.

But how pitiful it is to see so many liberals fall victim to the illusion that their ideals are best served by means which in truth would strangle these ideals! What a tragedy to see them embrace the idea that the quintessence of liberalism is something which is in reality the negation of the whole liberal heritage!

Yes, in the whole thousand-year-long history of liberalism there has never been any uncertainty as to the source of the overwhelmingly greatest danger to the rights, sovereignty, and inviolability of man. There was never any doubt that while there are many small, diffuse, special dangers to the dignity of every individual, there is only one single great concentrated danger to the dignity of all: the danger of strangulation by the organized power of the state. The fight for freedom, human rights, and human dignity has always consisted in restricting the power of that crushing thing the state, in balancing it and dividing it This was the whole proclaimed meaning of liberalism. All the struggles for freedom in history were struggles against the power of the state. In the last analysis they all amounted to conquering and preserving that simple indefinable thing which Justice Brandeis called the most fundamental of all rights: "The makers of the Constitution sought to protect Americans in their beliefs, their thoughts, their emotions, and their sensations. They conferred, as against the government, their right to be left alone— the most comprehensive of rights and the right most valued by civilized men."

What a spectacle to find so many liberals of our day following the exactly opposite path! They no longer erect walls against the state and defend them. They call upon us to tear down existing walls. They no longer try strictly to limit the zones to which the state has access; they invite it to supervise ever widening zones. They are furious against small, diffuse, special damages which they find anywhere or of which they only suspect the existence. Their sharpest attacks are directed against the "monopolies"—that is, against the biggest among the hundreds of thousands of employers. But to banish the real or imaginary sins of these monopolies, they call for a titanic super-monopoly which would combine the power of all the hundreds of thousands of employers and which represents all the great dangers in concentrated form. Liberalism is the descendant of the doctrine of "divided powers": let no power be totally in one hand! To-day, completely reversing this doctrine, the liberals desire to place in one hand the economic power which, thank God, is now divided among a hundred thousand; and, to place it in the very hand that already holds the political power. And all this for the sole purpose of achieving an extraordinary improvement in living standards—which again is imaginary! Is there no road back from this error? Can you no longer recognize the truth that the hundreds of thousands of employers, whatever the sins of any one of them, are still incomparably more bearable than would be one single total employer? Is it still not clear that a thing can be bad, but its opposite immeasurably worse? The faith in the saving virtues of the opposite has in our lifetime led to an unprecedented catastrophe; it led mankind directly into a new war instead of into the hoped-for perpetual peace. Are we destined to discover that the faith in the opposite will through a new direct development bring servitude to mankind instead of the hoped-for higher freedom?

Abundance for all: what an alluring aim! It cannot be achieved more successfully through socialistic methods than through "free enterprise." But even if it could be, do not lose sight of the price! Let not this one passion, this one desire, this one appetite rob mankind of all sense to such a point that it takes the risk of giving the state all power over every man's subsistence—or even over most of it. Then once again Edmund Burke's dictum will be confirmed: "Men are qualified for civil liberty in exact proportion to their disposition to put chains upon their own appetites. . . . It is ordained in the eternal constitution of things that men of intemperate habits cannot be free. Their passions forge their fetters." Should the passion for gigantic economic progress lead to the plunge into economic omnipotence for the state or to anything approximating it, fetters would be forged of which the innocent do not suspect the true nature. A cruel historical irony will materialize: the "total state," against whose power victory has been won on the battlefield, will after the war be admitted through the back door.

Let us, therefore, remember the truth that man's well-being is composed of many elements. Let us not forget that what seems to favour one element can be fatal to another. Let us not sacrifice one in order to improve another, let alone to improve it in a purely imaginary fashion. And least of all let freedom be the sacrificed element! If after this war destiny mercifully asks us the Shakespearian question: "What is't thou canst demand?"

let our answer be, first and foremost, now and always: "Our liberty!"

Let us agree that *the government's power over the means of production means its power over everyone's subsistence. Its power over this sounds the knell of individual freedom.*

CONCLUSION

CIVILIZATION TENDS TO conceal that which is the supreme necessity of all life. The realization that life is a perpetual struggle for self-preservation is growing weaker. The mind of man is concentrated on possible improvements of the world, not on defence against deterioration. What he already has he takes for granted. He likens history to the climbing of a mountain: every height he attains he feels is attained definitely, and his thoughts are turned to the next stage of the ascent. This is the progressivist conception of the world.

Unfortunately, the true picture is one of constantly raging struggle. "*Vivere, mi Lucili, militare est*," said Seneca. To live is to fight. Nothing that has been achieved by the individual, by the nation, or by society is ever safe. Everything material or immaterial is always in danger of being lost again. The struggle is never finished, and it demands by far the greatest part of man's activity. Every thought about the embellishment of life must be paid for with ten anxieties over the preservation of life. To make it possible for one effort to be directed toward the birth of a better world, ten efforts must be directed toward the prevention of a worse one. And, although usually the fact is not recognized, this struggle is for the greatest of all stakes. For the rights, freedom, and wealth we already possess are altogether more precious than what the future may add to them. What must be defended against destruction is a greater treasure than any improvements that may be made.

Very well, then, self-preservation is the first thing we shall attain by this war. And there is no reason for disdaining it. Far from it! The fact alone that the most brutal, most total deterioration has been prevented in the face of the most rabid of all attacks would be a precious gain. It would be worth all the sacrifices we are making. Even if no better world were born after this conflict, we should be wrong to minimize the successful prevention of a worse one with a querulous "Is that all?"

But that is not all. If no serious mistakes are made, a further achievement over and above this primary objective is equally certain. And through this second achievement we shall really enter a better world. Mankind can render Germany and Japan completely harmless for generations. And it so happens that Germany and Japan have caused not only the present war. For generations they alone have caused all the great wars. Since 1815 all wars between coalitions of great powers have been German wars. Since 1859, all wars between individual great powers have been German or Japanese wars. From a practical, although not from a philosophical point of view, it can be said that after Napoleon I no world war would have taken place if Germany had been without arms; and that after Napoleon III no duel between two great powers would have taken place if Germany and Japan had both been without arms. The military elimination of these two powers will not mean the absolute elimination of every war, but it will exclude any wars caused by those nations that in the past have actually initiated all the great wars. Should not a world in which this is achieved be considered a better world?

The popular answer to this question is: No. In the popular mind, a future deserving the epithet "better" must in some respects be not only better, but perfect. Universal peace must be realized, and something very close to permanent well-being. Most people are extremely confident of the possibility of achieving these goals; and at the same time they are terrified of a future in which these goals might not be achieved. "Wee follow and gape after future, uncertaine and unknowne things," wrote Montaigne four hundred years ago, "because the present and knowne doe not satisfie us. Man supposing it is the vice and fault of the things he possesseth, feedeth and filleth himself with other things, which he neither knoweth, nor hath understanding of, whereto he applyeth both his desires and hopes. As saith Cæsar: It happneth by the common fault of nature that wee are both more confident of and more terrified by things unseene, things hidden and things unknowne." Any success in these things, whether great or small, depends upon man's approaching them in a spirit that is neither too confident nor too terrified.

It is not an exaggerated hope that in the fields of universal peace and permanent well-being, also, great things will prove attainable. But in order to make them attainable our ideas about them must remain moderate. The world has the prospect of a long peace and of progressively greater well-being if it does not fall victim to the illusion of absolute and total solutions. A better future can be realized if we do not insist that the maximum must be realized and if things certain and known are not sacrificed for things "uncertaine and unknowne."

Yes, there are very real possibilities in matters of war and peace. If the big cloud that still remains, the cloud of Russian expansion, mercifully passes, a good measure of hope is justified. And, fortunately, this is not a hope which can materialize only if a world authority proves workable. The difference between a world with and without a world authority is not so overwhelming as the fantasies of the naïve would have us believe. In the form in which such an authority is a practical possibility—that is, as an association of countries in full possession of their own military power—it will in essence be no more than the promise of its members—really of the big three—to be faithful guardians. Now, there is a certain force in every promise. Better a promise than no promise. But the mere fact that the promise can at any time be circumvented or broken by everyone, will constantly compel all concerned to caution, reservations, and reassurances. As a result, the world authority will not be an Olympus beyond the reach of earthly cares nor, on the other hand, a mechanical robot. To a great extent it will only be another framework for struggles such as have always taken place without this framework: struggles for balancing and usefully grouping the powers. What the world authority can or cannot achieve will, in large measure, be only the result of the policies which, with more or less intelligence and resolution, are fought out among its members.

The result of all this can be peace, and the existence of the world authority as a framework may help somewhat. But this desired result is neither secured by the existence of such a framework nor precluded by the non-existence of such a framework. The same intelligence and resolution which will have to do the work within the world authority will have a chance without it. In brief, a wise policy is always the important thing. An astonishing lack of political wisdom lost the peace between 1919 and 1939, despite the existence of a world authority. A minimum of political wisdom would have preserved it even without a world authority. The key to the situation is not promises or mechanisms, but intelligence.

There is no longer any obscurity as to what intelligence requires from nations which want peace: they must be strong and on the alert. They must not put their faith in phrases and sermons, and must be ready for risks and sacrifices. They must begin their repressions when danger first shows itself, not after it has fully blossomed. Although they follow their own interests, they must follow their large, not their petty interests. They must be capable of recognizing at any moment which country is and which country is not dangerous. They must pursue the policy of the balance of power—which is eternal!—in favour of the non-dangerous countries, and not foolishly and blindly in favour of the dangerous ones. And at the critical moment they must be on the spot, ready to help and to spend themselves—for he who tries to keep aloof weakens the prospects of peace to the extent of his strength. If the intelligence required by such a policy is present, peace will have a better chance than ever whether the world authority is a success or a failure. It should be possible to preserve the peace, if not absolutely and mechanically, at least practically, and at least long enough to spare the present generation any more horrors.

Even better are the prospects for increasing human welfare and well-being; and let us place moral welfare and moral well-being foremost. Certainly, only the will of men forges their destiny, including that part of it which can be called their moral welfare. No world settlement can dictate in what direction the nations should develop their civilization and ethics and customs. This is inconceivable in actuality and if democracy is to mean anything. Victory will give every country the opportunity to return to the standards of dignity and freedom, wherever they were achieved before, and to strive for those standards wherever they have not yet been attained. The use the nations make of this opportunity can be influenced only little. But practically there is no reason for doubting that good use will be made of it in many parts of the world. Practically there is only one great danger. That is the widespread belief that some predetermined "trend," some inescapable "force," some irresistible "law of development" of our epoch demands that the governments be made omnipotent and that we be delivered over to them in bondage. Only if this tragic belief prevails, or provokes too violent struggles, will the prospect of a new flowering of moral welfare vanish. Let us do what we can to check this tragic belief.

And let us at the same time secure the basis for the best possible economic development. For precisely from the economic point of view a better world is as good as certain, provided it is not expected too sanguinely to be a perfect world. The period of transition after the war, the terrifying years of confusion, of re-organization, and, to a large extent, of hunger and chaos, promise to be shorter and easier than the pessimists imagine. Every era's capacity for reconstruction and reorganization corresponds with its capacity for destruction and disorganization. A world in which a wise policy no longer permits the peace to degenerate into a farce will constitute more fertile soil for an economic flowering such as has not been experienced for a long time. "*Faites-moi de bonne politique, et je vous ferai de bonnes finances!*" ("Give me a sound policy, and I will give you sound finances!") Baron Louis exclaimed to Louis Philippe, and what is true of finances is true of all branches of economic life. Do away with the barriers that split up this soil. Let the millions of profit-seekers bring forth the results that they brought forth throughout generations. Let the servant state add what could not be achieved by their methods. The balance will be earthly but good; not a miracle, but a trinity of constantly rising living standards, elementary security, and fully preserved rights and freedoms.

To be sure, in the perspective of this better future there is an "if." In things human there are inevitably only conditional possibilities. These possibilities are real only if man takes advantage of them and only if he does not sooner or later spoil them. To create guarantees that he will not ruin them is impossible. The better future means a number of possibilities with the reservations of this great "if." Furthermore, the possibilities are imperfect. The nature of the old Adam is dual, the nature of things is full of contradictions. There are no absolute solutions for anything; there is always only a perfectible balance between divergent necessities. The possibilities of a better future, already subject to the great "if," are, in addition, limited. In all honesty nobody can promise more than that.

Few things are more annoying than the defeatism of those who are clamouring for just the things nobody can honestly promise, and who fall into whining desperation when in answer to their constant questions about the "meaning of the war" they are shown not heaven but only the earth. It is on the earth that we are living. With all possible improvements and diminished imperfections it will still remain the earth. No generation is entitled to expect that for its benefit something entirely novel should suddenly be made of the earth; and it is hard to be patient with complainers who behave as though the earth were hell.

Are they not infected to an alarming extent with that modern *vice allemand* which has already spoiled the life of mankind, that obsessive taking offence at the most normal, most unavoidable shortcomings of existence, that eternal wailing, querulous, self-pitying attitude of complaint? Let us not make the earth fouler than it is! Even in the past it gave us a life from which, despite all the worries, tasks, and suffering that were inseparable from our joys, delights, and accomplishments, only few departed willingly. This will not change; this was not and is not horrible. And there is still no better wisdom than that of Ecclesiastes: a man should rejoice in his works, and eat and drink, and enjoy the good of all the labour that he taketh under the sun all the days of his life which God giveth him: for that is his portion.